THE GOSPEL OF CUSTOMER SERVICE

O. Bernard Smalls

Timeless Principles of Customer Service

hanks God it's Sunday! www.bernardsmalls.com

THE GOSPEL OF CUSTOMER SERVICE

DEDICATED TO:

Dr. Ken and Margie Blanchard

Thanks, Ken and Margie, for showing so many of us the way. Your teachings and example have had a tremendous and positive impact on my life. The two weeks I spent in your home were certainly life changing. You are both definitely loving teachers of simple truths that awaken the presence of God in us. This book could not exist without your generous spirits.

THE GOSPEL OF CUSTOMER SERVICE

CONTENTS

Chapter 1:	TGI-SUNDAY!	Page 4
Chapter 2:	Java Time	Page 09
Chapter 3:	Monday, Monday!	Page 10
Chapter 4:	Crunch Time…gotta have a job!	Page 13
Chapter 5:	A Great Day at Excellent Way!	Page 14
Chapter 6:	The Waiting Game!	Page 21
Chapter 7:	Training Day—One Commitment to Excellence	Page 23
Chapter 8:	Destined for Greatness	Page 28
Chapter 9:	The Three Spiritual Principles A Meaningful Service Vision	Page 33
Chapter 10:	Training Day—Two Customer-Oriented People	Page 44
Chapter 11:	Training Day—Three	Page 63
Chapter 12:	TGI–SUNDAY! Again!	Page 80

THE GOSPEL OF CUSTOMER SERVICE

GREATNESS!
No one achieves greatness without being of service. Service is the essence of greatness. All great man and women are great because they first gave some talent or ability in service to others. And no matter how small our talent, we too can contribute in some way to others—we too can become GREAT!

THE GOSPEL OF CUSTOMER SERVICE

CHAPTER 1

"TGI – SUNDAY!"

      This book is a journey into the potential for greatness in you! Yes, you have the potential for greatness.
      I firmly believe that deep within each human being is the question, "What makes the great great?" As you read this book, I believe you will discover that the real key to true greatness is to be of service to others. No matter who you are, if you are breathing you are in customer service in one way or another. The concept of service is misunderstood by most people. Whether you are Michael Jordan, Wayne Gretzky, Billy Graham, or Jim Moran—the founder of Southeast Toyota who literally changed the face of the automotive business—or simply a janitor, you are in customer service. What do all the great ones have in common? (By the way, Wayne Gretzky was called "the great one.") They have an attitude of being of service instead of being self-serving. They all served their audiences or customers with impeccable excellence and became great.
      You can be a shining star if you learn how to serve others with excellence. You need to read this book and reap the life-changing benefits of delivering excellent service. I have lived it! As they say, "Been there; done that!"
By the way, this book really has nothing to do with religion as most people understand religion. It's really about the true religion of being kind to others and serving them with excellence in every way, whether at home, at work, at the marketplace, at the church or the synagogue, or even in the world of entertainment. So relax! If you are a coffee drinker, I want you to know that great coffee and this book are extremely compatible. ⊠
Read and enjoy, while I introduce you to some everyday people and profound concepts that will bring you true wealth and greatness through service.

…IT'S SUNDAY!

THE GOSPEL OF CUSTOMER SERVICE

Joseph Simple and his friend, Zack Billiard, pulled up in Joe's new BMW to the contemporary corporate headquarters building and saw a mass of excited people passing through the large, beautiful entry into the butterfly-shaped pavilion. Some were wearing jeans, some wore shorts, while others were conservatively casual. They were young, elderly, black, white, Asian, Hispanic—you name it. This place is the best diversity training I have ever had, thought Joe.

The one constant that captured Joe's attention was the enthusiasm they all seemed to have. After they were seated, the band started playing some upbeat contemporary music and Joe leaned over and said to his friend Zack, "This is different." Zack just looked at him with a big smile and said, "Thanks for coming with me today, Joe."

They sang three songs, along with the band and then the minister, who was comfortably, but well-dressed in a dark blue sports coat with a black turtleneck, came to the pulpit and sat down. After a young, attractive teenaged soloist had finished her song, the minister stood up and said to the congregation, "Good morning, and welcome to our service!"

The minister then said to the congregation, "Now let's all say 'TGIS,' which means THANK GOD IT'S SUNDAY!" After this affirmation, you could hear light laughter and enthusiastic chuckles ignite throughout the beautiful non-religious church auditorium. People obviously felt good about being there.

The minister then proclaimed, "Today's sermon is entitled, 'The Gospel of Customer Service.' My thesis is 'The Call to Wealth.'" As he opened his message, he asked the crowd "Did you know that the word gospel literally means good news or a good message? The good news is that excellent customer service is not just for Sunday. It's for every day!"

"A message on customer service may seem like a strange title for a Sunday morning service, but remember, the good news is not just for Sunday. I preach a positive theology because people don't need to hear how bad they are; they need to hear how good God is. They need to hear good

THE GOSPEL OF CUSTOMER SERVICE

news. A part of that good news is financial prosperity and greatness for those who learn how to serve others with excellence.

"Many people don't understand the importance of the practical issue of service. I believe that excellent service is directly linked to the financial prosperity of an organization or a business. Financial prosperity in an organization is in direct proportion to how it takes care of customers, partners, members and markets. As my good friend Ken Blanchard puts it, 'Profit is the applause we get for taking care of our customers.'

"God gives us the power to create wealth. Even Socrates said,

> "Wealth does not bring goodness, but goodness brings wealth and every other blessing, both to the individual and the state."
> - Socrates

Wealth can be enjoyed by understanding this practical and spiritual message of making a 100% commitment to the simple, yet profound concept of excellent customer service!"

The minister continued. "Nordstrom became a favorite shopping spot when I lived in the Northwest. At one time, for approximately five years straight, I visited Nordstrom at least once a week to buy a shirt, a tie, or just to get a fresh hot cup of Seattle's Best Coffee. John W. Nordstrom started his business in the early 1900s with a vision of outstanding customer service that has continued to grow for more than a century."

The minister went on to say, "I was reading a book recently that explained the gospel according to Nordstrom by the following phrase: This is why we are here—to serve and be kind!"

"Reportedly, one delighted customer went so far as to stipulate in her will that her ashes be scattered at Nordstrom. 'That way,' she said, 'I am certain my children will visit me often.'" The minister told the congregation that the challenge to be of service or to be extraordinarily kind brings out the best in everybody.

THE GOSPEL OF CUSTOMER SERVICE

"In my estimation, Nordstrom is certainly a great customer service organization. How many of you have shopped at Nordstrom?" Many hands went up. Several people leaned over to the person seated next to them and whispered the impact Nordstrom had had on them. "Nordstrom is committed to 100% guaranteed customer satisfaction."

"In my years as a corporate trainer, I found that all great organizations have a certain mindset about excellent customer service. Their central focus is always the customer. I believe it is high time that we learn the good virtues from the great organizations and then take it to another level through God's great love for humanity."

"This may be challenging for the super 'religious' folks, but God said in Luke 16: 8, 'The children of this world are in their generation wiser than the children of light.' Why did God say they are wiser? When it comes to dealing in the everyday practical affairs of business and making money, the children of this age are often wiser than the average religious Joe." The minister proclaimed, "The Gospel of Customer Service is simply wisdom and common sense. However, Zig Ziglar says, 'Common sense is not always common practice!'"

"I know it's obvious that I am really passionate about customer service. If you were to take a knife and cut me open, customer service excellence would bleed out of me. But don't try it; I don't like the sight of blood."

The late Henry Ford was passionate about taking care of customers. He certainly had it right when it came to customer service. He said,

> "If We Are Not Customer-Driven, Then Our Cars Won't Be Either!"
>
> Henry Ford

The minister asked, "Does God know anything about service?" A handsome, heavy set, well-dressed, black gentleman in the normally calm auditorium shouted, "Amen, bro!"

THE GOSPEL OF CUSTOMER SERVICE

Let me use a theological phrase for emphasis. Many customer service representatives need to repent and believe the Gospel of Customer Service. We have all seen customer-endearing signs at businesses such as:

> **MANAGEMENT RESERVES THE RIGHT TO REFUSE SERVICE TO ANYBODY!**

> **NO CHANGES OR SUBSTITUTIONS ALLOWED!**

> **ALL SALES ARE FINAL!**

Remember, we are talking about the Gospel (good news) of Customer Service; not calling down fire and brimstone on people who bring us complaints."
"There are three major factors or principles that, when understood and properly implemented, make an organization excellent in customer service. You could call these the triple bottom line to super customer service."

The three spiritual principles are:

1. A Meaningful Service VISION
2. Customer-Oriented PEOPLE
3. Customer-Friendly SYSTEMS

The minister summarized and concluded his sermon by saying, "The good news is that we all can improve on our customer service, be better family members and citizens, and have a positive affect in our world. A customer is simply anyone who depends on you to get a need met. The Gospel of Customer Service is great because it fulfils the golden rule:
Do unto others as you would have them do unto you!"

# THE GOSPEL OF CUSTOMER SERVICE

CHAPTER 2

"JAVA TIME"

Joe Simple, formerly a successful C.T.O. (Chief Technology Officer), had been invited to church to hear the pastor's sermon on The Gospel of Customer Service by Zack, a former co-worker. After church, they stopped by the local Starbucks to have a couple of flavored lattes. As they sat and sipped the gourmet coffee, Aretha Franklin's R.E.S.P.E.C.T. played in the background and people were lined up at the counter awaiting their java fixes.

Zack asked Joe,

"Well, did you enjoy the service?"

Joe said, "Funny that you should ask. I know I've been a little quiet, but it's because I've been pondering the whole experience. To say the least, it was different. I was raised Episcopalian and was not quite prepared for all of the contemporary stuff and the message on wealth in church. The whole thing just didn't seem religious enough for me. The minister didn't even wear a tie or a robe, and that blew me away. Plus, I had always been taught in church that poverty was a virtue. It all sounded good, but I have always been warned to look out for things that sound too good to be true. The people were all very nice and everything was excellent, especially the music. In fact, I felt a little guilty for enjoying the rhythm section of the band. I expected a choir with a grand piano and not the Atlanta Rhythm Section. Yet I must say there were a lot of young and elderly people there that seemed to be getting a lot out of this non-religious approach to church. I am still weighing the whole experience."

Zack saw that this was going nowhere and this was no time to put the pressure on. Joe needed time to sort it all out.

Zack simply replied, "Interesting comments. Thanks for the feedback. Do you want another shot of java, Joe?" Joe yelled to the girl behind the counter to bring two more rounds of the same.

The young lady smiled and enthusiastically replied

"My pleasure!"

THE GOSPEL OF CUSTOMER SERVICE

CHAPTER 3

"MONDAY, MONDAY"

It was Monday morning and Joe Simple woke up at 4:00 a.m. in a cold sweat. He was worried about how he would maintain his standard of living. The 9/11 terrorist attacks and the subsequent layoffs at Quality Plus—an Atlanta based technology communications firm—had put him in a challenging financial position after losing his six figure income, benefits and position as Chief Technology Officer.

As he pondered his situation, his mind went back to the minister's sermon, especially the part about the call to wealth. Joe had visited the church to repay a favor to Zack. Zack knew Joe's concerns about his financial future since the layoff and thought the minister's message could be his answer. Joe had been a hit-or-miss church go-er, and not quite what you would call "a fan" of spiritual things. He had a casual approach to religion and believed it was a personal issue, not one that should be discussed in public. He had a real distaste for anything that resembled a religious fanatic.

As Joe lay in the bed this Monday morning, he thought deeply on the sermon. It seemed that the pastor's words kept ringing in his heart. He looked over at his wife, who was sound asleep, and decided to get up and brew some fresh coffee. While having a hot cup of Starbuck's coffee, he picked up and started looking through the local paper. As he glanced through the want ads, he saw an ad in the sales section that said

> **"OPPORTUNITY FOR BIG BUCKS"**
> *70 – 190K Annually*
> *Please call Oscar at*
> **EXCELLENT WAY AUTOMOTIVE GROUP**
> *770.555.1234*

THE GOSPEL OF CUSTOMER SERVICE

Joe looked at the pay and thought, That's too good to be true! Nobody can possibly make that kind of money selling cars. Joe had seen the movies "Suckers" and "Used Cars" and thought they depicted the totality of the car sales profession. He thought they were all car dogs! He thought to himself, The reputation of a car salesman is not the image I want. They are all scumbags. How can I go from being a Chief Technology Officer to being a car salesmen? That would be like selling your soul to the devil. They are like liars that create more and more lies everyday to rip off innocent people. The scum of the earth... Then Joe caught himself and said, "Man, you're getting negative. The layoff and consequent financial situation is getting to you mentally and emotionally. I guess all car salesmen are not car dogs." He jotted down the number in his day-timer and continued to look for I.T. jobs.

Joe saw that the section on I.T. positions had shrunk to just a few lines. Each one he called had filled the position and was still receiving an average of 7,500 resumés a day through monster.com, the mail, and other sources. He kept looking at job ads for the rest of the morning. At noon, in desperation and looking at his dwindling savings account, he decided he would call the number of the car dealership after lunch.

Joe had worked part-time in car sales for a car dealership when he did his undergrad studies at Atlanta University and while completing his MBA at Georgia Business Technology Institute. It was okay for a college job, but he never thought he would end up in the car business again. Besides, he was looking into the New Age Religion, seeking to find his spiritual footing in life, and realized that his experience in the auto business was not the image he had of being a good, ethical and peaceful person. As far as morality and quality of life were concerned, well... the movies "Suckers" and "Used Cars" just kept running through his mind. I can't do this, he thought as he looked at the OPPORTUNITY FOR BIG BUCKS ad again. Immediately, he became doubtful. "Yeah, I bet this whole thing is a front. They are probably just a group of greedy crooks." Joe kept looking in the classified ads, only to find that lucrative I.T. jobs were few and far between since the 9/11 attacks. What am I going to do? he wondered. I just can't bow that low to be a car salesman.

THE GOSPEL OF CUSTOMER SERVICE

The image of the fat, fast talking, lying, cigarette smoking car salesperson is just not who I am. I'll just wait it out. I bet we will catch that stupid Ben Ladin and all of this terrorism stuff will blow over, so that once again we can enjoy the "good old I.T. days." I just can't call that dealership. He went on-line, only to find more of the same thing- layoffs, downsizing, closures and unemployment rates increasing. He said, "I still have some savings and 401K money. I'll just tough it out."

THE GOSPEL OF CUSTOMER SERVICE

CHAPTER 4

"CRUNCH TIME"

Six months later, Joe had called every I.T. ad, followed every lead and networked every contact he could find to no avail. Savings were dwindling and desperation was setting in. Things were only getting worse in the once money-spinning I.T. industry. You could say the game had changed after 9/11. He went back to the drawer into which he had thrown the EXCELLENT WAY AUTOMOTIVE GROUP ad, only to find the "OPPORTUNITY FOR BIG BUCKS" caption staring him in the face. He thought, Even if this is a hoax, it's crunch time. I am ready to give it a try to generate some cash flow. He humorously thought, At least it would be better than making a "Will Work for Food" sign.

He called the dealership and was amazed at how pleasant, cheerful and professional the receptionist was. She answered, "It's a Great Day at Excellent Way! How can I serve you?"
Joe said, "Wow, what a greeting! I am calling about the ad in the paper for salespersons."
The receptionist said, "Great. Our sales people are some of my favorite people in the world. I'll connect you to Mr. Oscar Paywell's office. He does the interviewing and hiring." Oscar's administrative assistant thanked Joe for calling and told him how business was booming and how they needed more sales professionals. Joe could hardly believe business could be so great for Excellent Way while the I.T. field was experiencing such a slump.
Joe asked,
   "How could business possibly be booming?"
The assistant replied, "Mr. Simple, our business is always good due to our strong customer service positioning. We believe that if you take care of customers in the good times, they will honor you with their patronage during the lean times. In addition to this, interest rates are at an all-time low since the terrorist attacks, so you could say it is a buyer's market. Finally, this area is the fastest growing area in the country, second only to Vegas.
Joe thought, A-ha. Even Vegas might not be a bad idea right now.

He set up an appointment for an interview with Oscar for Thursday of the same week. On Thursday morning, Joe jumped into one of his best conservative corporate suits with a white shirt and tie, hopped into his BMW and headed to EXCELLENT WAY to meet Oscar.

THE GOSPEL OF CUSTOMER SERVICE

CHAPTER 5

"A GREAT DAY AT EXCELLENT WAY"

As Joe pulled up to the gate of the dealership, he was shocked to see that a valet literally came running to his car, saying, "It's a great day AT EXCELLENT WAY! Thanks for visiting us. How can we serve you?"
Joe asked, "What's up with the security gate and the valet service? Is this the CHEESECAKE FACTORY or a car dealership?"
The valet replied, "Great sense of humor, sir. We are committed to the Gospel of Customer Service here. Our mission statement is TO SERVE THE MORE EXCELLENT WAY.' We do our best to make sure our customers have a great experience. Even if they don't buy an automobile, we want to help brighten their day by the EXCELLENT WAY experience." While the valet was still talking, a luxury golf cart came zooming around the corner. The driver, a very pleasant Haitian man, greeted and picked up Joe and took him to the foyer of the executive offices. Joe tried to give the driver a tip, but the driver said, "No, thank you, sir. We are here to give to our guests, not take from them. Enjoy your day at EXCELLENT WAY! Here is my card with my two-way radio number and here is a radio for you. If you need me to take you anywhere on the grounds, feel free to page me or press 000 for the operator and she will be glad to page me."
Joe was stunned and walked away, shaking his head. As he walked up to the entry of the foyer, the thought hit him, Wow, and I'm just here for an interview. I wonder how they treat their customers?

As he walked up to the door, he could not help but notice how excellent and beautiful everything was. The signs were all brightly painted and strategically placed to give the customers directions. The lawn and flowers were absolutely immaculate. All of the people were especially nice, including the lawn crew and porters. He immediately noticed that there were no eardrum-piercing pages from the sales desk for people out on the lot. Instead, they all had two-way radios. Even the lot attendants and the lawn crew communicated with two-way radios. His image of the car business was gradually changing. Could this be real, or is it just a front to get people in? I know the drill, Joe thought. There is always a hook in the bait. This is probably just a part of their bait-and-switch tactic. You know, fatten them up for the kill.

THE GOSPEL OF CUSTOMER SERVICE

Joe walked up to the automatic sliding doors and was met by a lovely, pleasant female greeter who said, "IT'S A GREAT DAY AT EXCELLENT WAY! How can I serve you?"

"I'm here to see Oscar Paywell for an interview."

"Great. I will page him. Please have a seat, sir. Mr. Paywell will be with you shortly."

Joe sat in the huge, comfortable, all-leather chair near the greeter's station and enjoyed the smooth jazz as he looked at all the beautiful art work and many awards that EXCELLENT WAY had earned.

"Oscar is just wrapping up a meeting, Mr. Simple. Would you like a beverage while you wait?"

Joe said, "I'll take a diet coke, please."

"Coming right up!" the greeter said as she picked up the phone to contact the dealership's in-house deli. The waiter from the deli came, dressed in a tux, with a large cup of ice and two diet cokes with lemon. Joe said, "Wow, is this the Ritz Carlton?"

The waiter smiled and said, "We want to make it a GREAT DAY at EXCELLENT WAY for all of our guests."

Joe thought, This all looks good on the front, but I bet there's a snake in the bushes somewhere, and I'll find it. Car dealerships are all about CASH. When I was working part-time in a dealership in college, my sales manager continually said CASH IS KING! You know, fatten them up and put the knife in them.

While Joe waited, he thought, I'll bet the restrooms are not as excellent. I was told in a training class that the condition of the restrooms tells the truth about the business.

As Joe walked on the luxurious wood floors in the hallway to go to the restrooms, he was astonished by the responsiveness of all of the support staff and sales personnel, who were all excellently dressed in blue and gold. He had always been taught that car sales people are just sales dogs who are only friendly to people who put cash in their pockets.

THE GOSPEL OF CUSTOMER SERVICE

As Joe approached the restroom door, he smiled and thought Now is the moment of truth. As he touched the door, it opened electronically and he immediately heard the classical music and smelled the strawberry air freshener that was being sprayed in a mist through ceiling ducts. The beautiful oak trimming and soft lighting made it a rich experience. An attendant dressed in blue and gold was stationed in the men's room to provide assistance to any guest in need. The attendant, a handsome middle-aged man, said "IT'S A GREAT DAY AT EXCELLENT WAY! Thanks for visiting us." Joe walked up to the sink to freshen up and noticed every kind of hygiene item you would need or desire, including mouthwash, disposable toothbrushes and toothpaste. There were also small samples of men's cologne for a little touch up. He washed his hands and looked for the disposable towels. He was surprised that the counter was stacked with real cloth towels and a large, beautiful wicker basket nearby to toss the used ones. Above the towels was a sign with the current date that read, "EXCELLENT WAY THOUGHT FOR THE DAY:. Only The Best For Our Guests And YOU Are the Best!" Joe walked out of the rest room, literally scratching and shaking his head.

As soon as Joe returned to his diet coke and took a seat in the large comfortable leather chair, Oscar Paywell came out, with a bounce in his step. Also conservatively and excellently dressed in blue and gold, with a cheerful smile, he said, "You must be Mr. Simple. Thanks for coming in today. IT'S A GREAT DAY AT EXCELLENT WAY! I'm Oscar Paywell, the Apostle of Customer Service and the C.E.O. of EXCELLENT WAY AUTOMOTIVE GROUP."

Joe said, "I guess so!" as he nearly choked. Joe was a little shocked by Oscar's boldness to identify himself as an Apostle.

Oscar said, "Don't let the word apostle throw you; it simply means one sent on a mission. I am on a mission of changing the customer service in the automotive industry. I have been looking forward to meeting you. Let's go to my office."

Oscar had the greeter page a waiter from the deli to bring Joe's partially finished diet coke, along with a fresh drink and some extra lemons, to his office.
Joe said, "Mr. Paywell, before we get started I want to ask you something."
"Go right ahead," said Oscar. "But please call me Oscar."

THE GOSPEL OF CUSTOMER SERVICE

Joe said, "I know this may sound kind of dumb, but why am I in the executive offices for an interview to be a sales person?"

Oscar said, "It's not a dumb question at all. I get it all the time. The answer is simple. We believe in delivering outstanding customer service to every guest. You are a guest, Joe. Everyone that drives up or walks onto this property is treated like a guest, a king, or a queen. Besides that, I am the primary owner and I like to hand pick my sales consultants because they represent me as they interact with our customers. I invite them into my world so they can see what the heart and the head of our business is like, instead of into some dingy interview room. First, we believe in our people. We like to make people feel special, and there is nothing special about a grimy interview or training room.

"We also understand the power of first impressions. In fact, take a look at this." He pointed to a beautifully framed motivational quote that said "You Never Get a Second Chance to Make a First Impression."

"By the way, that was a gift from my good friend, Peter J. Daniels, who is an extremely successful Australian Spiritual Entrepreneur."

The thought Spiritual Entrepreneur lingered in Joe's mind during the rest of the interview and during the tour of the facilities. A spiritual entrepreneur is a business owner that leads from the heart—the gut, if you would. They lead and live from the inside out. This reminded Joe of the concepts in the sermon he had heard when he visited Zack's church several months earlier.

Joe followed Oscar past his executive desk to a handsome round oak table in the south end of his office, where they sat down. He noticed a beautiful poster that said:

Commitment to Excellence

"The quality of a man's life will be in his direct proportion to his commitment to excellence, no matter what his chosen field of endeavor is."

- Vince Lombardi

THE GOSPEL OF CUSTOMER SERVICE

Oscar said, "Thanks for coming in for an interview, Joe. Feel free to help yourself to the cookies and finger foods." After a little more small talk and rapport building, Oscar got right down to business. "Joe, I am a Spiritual Entrepreneur. That is why I humorously introduced myself as the Apostle of Customer Service. We here at Excellent Way are in the religion of service."

Joe said, "You sure did get my attention with that greeting. What does this spiritual stuff have to do with business and customer service?"

Oscar said, "Let me explain. I operate my store by practical and spiritual principles. You don't have to be religious to work here, but we look for people with great hearts—hearts of customer service."

"I believe that as a Spiritual Entrepreneur I am called to wealth, and I use that wealth to take care of my family, serve humanity and those in need."

Joe thought, This stuff sounds familiar, but he kept silent about his visit to his friend's church.

Oscar continued, "If this sounds good to you so far, let me carry on. If not, we can terminate the interview and part as friends."

Joe said, "Oh no, Mr. Paywell. I find this interesting. It reminds me of a church I attended a few months ago."

Oscar said, "Joe, call me Oscar, please. Don't make me feel old. Here are some hard-noised research-based facts about American Businesses."

- More than half of all businesses in the U.S. are service-related and those who perform best will dominate the market in the coming years.
- Men, women and children are no longer subject to the whims of product manufacturers.
- Companies today must provide quality products at a reasonable price just to stay in business. To thrive, companies must treat customers well.
- Few organizations, if any, can thrive today without repeat business. That means that any organization that wants to survive must not only attract new customers, but also keep existing customers excited.

THE GOSPEL OF CUSTOMER SERVICE

Oscar smiled and said softly, "Joe, Spiritual Entrepreneurs are really in the life-changing business. We create wealth and make money to help others. Because of this, we take business very seriously."

Joe responded, "Well, I am a relatively good person, but not a religious person per se. I used to attend the Episcopalian Church regularly in New Jersey, but since moving to Atlanta, I have let it slip. But you know, Oscar, I have been thinking about my spiritual journey a lot lately. I even went to this contemporary church with a friend recently, but I don't want to be a religious freak. I just want to enjoy peace of mind and prosperity for my family."

Oscar said, "I like what I'm feeling, Joe. This could be the place for you, but let me ask you some very important questions." Oscar pulled out a formal interview sheet and asked Joe twelve questions that were designed to find out his motivation, his energy and his ethics.

Joe responded with sweaty palms and wondered if he was answering right. Not to mention his concern with the fact that he may not be spiritual enough to work for a Spiritual Entrepreneur. After the questions were all answered, Oscar pulled out his reading glasses and went over Joe's responses with a fine tooth comb.

After a brief period of silent reflection, Oscar said, "I like what I am sensing. How is the diet coke holding out? Do you need another beverage?"

"No thanks. One more and I'll float away."

Oscar said, "Please follow me." He led Joe to a computer to take a personality test. "Please sit at this terminal and complete the AVA test."

Joe felt the leather arms on the chair at the computer terminal and said, "That's good stuff."

Oscar said, "Only the best for our guests!"

Joe sat in the comfortable leather chair and then asked, "Oscar, what in the world is an AVA test? I have taken hundreds of tests on the job in the many training programs that Quality Plus required I attend in order to keep my I.T. certifications, but never an AVA."

THE GOSPEL OF CUSTOMER SERVICE

it's a test to show us your sales personality tendencies, your assertiveness and your maturity. AVA is an acronym for ACTIVITY VECTOR ANALYSIS." Oscar continued, "I am a trained Executive AVA Analyst. I will go over the numbers when you are through. When the test is over, just press the blue button on the keyboard and I'll be right there."

After the test, Oscar concluded the formal interview and let Joe know that he would be in contact as soon as the results from the standard pre-employment screens were in.

Joe couldn't help but notice the plaque over Oscar's door as they were both leaving. It said:

> "Fulfilled, happy customers are the lifeblood of a business."
> - Ritz Carlton

Oscar escorted Joe to the main exit door and beeped the porter on the NEXTEL to bring Joe's car up to the door.

Joe said, "Wow, this place is certainly world class."

Oscar said, "Thanks Joe, and by the way, here's my card."

As Joe was leaving the interview, he thought, This is interesting. This guy seems to be very spiritual; yet, very practical when it comes to business, and especially customer service. If the service to customers is in any way near how I was treated today, then I want this job. I never thought anything good could come out of a car dealership, but I was wrong. I think this guy is the real deal.

Joe left the interview and jumped into his BMW. He tried again to give the porter a tip. The guy refused and said with a smile, "I hope you enjoyed your brief stay at EXCELLENT WAY."

Joe said, "You folks are almost poetic and the service is first class."

The young man said, "Thanks, Mr. Simple. Great service is our pleasure."

He jumped in, turned on the air and headed straight for the local Starbucks to have his favorite drink, a venti, sugar-free, vanilla latte.

THE GOSPEL OF CUSTOMER SERVICE

CHAPTER 6

"THE WAITING GAME"

The following morning Joe sat in his kitchen, having coffee with his lovely wife. He was watching and listening to world events on CNN when out of the blue he blurted, "I want it!"

His wife asked, "You want what?"

"I'm sorry, honey. I just have my fingers crossed, anxiously hoping that I get the job at EXCELLENT WAY." He then sighed doubtfully, "I bet they won't call me. I'm such a heathen. They'll probably hire some religious fanatic. On the other hand, Oscar, the owner, did say at one point in the interview that he liked what he was sensing."

His wife responded, "Time will tell, honey. You are still my hero, whether you get the job or not. Joe, do you want some more coffee?"

"Yeah, a refill would be fine." Joe said to his wife, "You sure are in a serving mood lately. What's gotten into you?"

At 10:00 a.m. sharp the phone rang. Joe's wife looked at the caller I.D. and said, "Honey, honey! It's a call from EXCELLENT WAY!"

Joe ran across the room, nearly knocking her over, and grabbed the phone. "Joe Simple speaking!"

"Hi Joe. This is Oscar Paywell at EXCELLENT WAY AUTOMOTIVE GROUP. Joe, this morning while I was praying, I got a real peace about bringing you into the company. We meet every morning at 6:00 a.m. to pray for our families and for the business. After praying over those applicants, we agreed that you should come and work on our sales team."

Joe was excited and said, "Great! I'll take it. When do you want me there? Yesterday I bet."

Oscar said, "No. Just enjoy the weekend and we will see you on Monday morning at 9:00 a.m. for orientation and customer-service training."

Joe got off the phone and said, "Go, Joseph! Go, Joseph! Go, Joseph!" as he did a dance. He said, "Honey I got it!"

"Great!" said his wife. "I prayed yesterday with that Smalley guy on TV for peace and prosperity for our marriage and family."

Joe said, "Whatever you did, it worked. Let's go celebrate. How about a Starbuck's venti latte? Maybe a bottle of French wine... Let's go!"

THE GOSPEL OF CUSTOMER SERVICE

As they were driving, Joe started to wonder about the spiritual implication of all that was happening. First he thought, I'm really blessed to get this job. Then he thought, am I becoming a spiritual freak? Better slow down. He even had a concern about whether he was getting into a cult. He thought, What if this Oscar guy is some Jim Jones? He laughed at himself as he thought, I surely won't be drinking any Kool-Aid! Through it all, he was excited about the income opportunity for big bucks and thought, Everyone there was so nice. It surely can't be a cult!

His wife said, "Honey! You just passed Starbucks."

Joe said, "I'm sorry. I was in another world for a moment," as he wheeled his stylish BMW around to head back to Starbucks.

THE GOSPEL OF CUSTOMER SERVICE

CHAPTER 7

"TRAINING DAY - ONE"

Joe showed up on Monday morning at 8:30 a.m. sharp for the EXCELLENT WAY orientation and customer-service training. He thought it strange that a car dealership would put its sales people through customer-service training before teaching them anything about selling cars. As he reflected, he remembered Oscar telling him that customer-service training was first and foremost, and to be followed by their "TGI-Saturday, Twelve Steps to a Sale" class. Oscar clearly stated that his vision was service first and sales second." Joe thought the training concept was impressive and interesting.

As he walked into the beautifully decorated training room, his ears were filled with the wonderful sounds of smooth jazz. The music was piped through the high-quality stereo speakers. He also noticed the wonderful breakfast spread, the motivational pictures on the wall, the gigantic screen for a power-point presentation and four flip charts strategically placed. Joe thought to himself, Everything here is so first class. He said to one of the waiters assigned to keeping the breakfast fresh and serving the trainees, "This sure is first class for a car dealership."

The waiter smiled and said, "Thank you, Mr. Simple. First-class service is our pleasure."
Since Joe was plenty early, he got a plate of breakfast goodies and found the table with his name typed on the blue and gold nameplate. Joe sat down and began reading the orientation materials that were on the tables in front of his nameplate. He reflected on the title, "The Gospel of Customer Service." For a moment he thought it sounded kind of religious, but everything seemed heavenly anyway. Let's get it on...

Oscar Paywell came in and greeted the class with an enthusiastic "Good Morning!" and said, "You are God's best and we are thrilled to have you as a part of our team. How many of you enjoyed the breakfast?"

Joe said, "It was awesome! I'm still licking my chops."

"Great. Our chefs prepared a good old-fashioned breakfast especially for you. Tomorrow we will have the traditional continental breakfast, but today we wanted to give you a finger-licking treat to show our appreciation for your becoming a team member."

While Oscar was talking, two well-groomed men and a tall attractive woman came in and sat in the rear of the training room. Oscar welcomed them and told the group that he had invited three of the EXCELLENT WAY shining stars to meet with the new trainees. As soon as Oscar said "shining stars,"

THE GOSPEL OF CUSTOMER SERVICE

Earth, Wind & Fire was piped through the training room's BOSE sound system performing, "You Are A Shining Star." All of the trainees started to clap or whistle. "You will spend more time with them later in the training process. The first star I want you to meet is from our sales department; she is Sally Sellers."

Sally waved as they gave her a round of applause. She then shouted to the class, "By the way, I am the proud mother of the two best teenage boys in the universe!"

"The next gentleman is Tom Treadwell from the service department." The class again began to applaud as Tom smiled and waved.

"Last, but not least, from our parts department is George Goodwrench. We call him 'Good Hands George.'" The class once again began to applaud. Oscar complimented the class for being so Gung Ho in cheering others on. Oscar thanked the three service stars for coming in and told them they could return to their departments.

"You will learn some foundational concepts of Customer Service that could change your entire life during the next three days. The reason I say that is that we all have customers, no matter what we do for a living. A customer is simply anyone depending on you to get a need met. The old saying still stands; 'if you want to be successful find a need and meet it.' Here at EXCELLENT WAY we simply meet people's transportation needs.

If you buy into these principles of customer service, we will place you in the sales training class. If you don't, we simply part company in peace. Is that fair? We want people that buy into our customer service culture more than we want sales people who can sell a lot of cars. Our commitment to excellence has caused us to make a decision not to have a sales staff of car dogs. We want people who will put our customers first and serve them like they would want to be served if they were purchasing an automobile. Some of the local dealerships have even made fun of how they abuse customers by lying about things like the trade-in value, the interest rates, and the price of the vehicle, and then they say, 'The devil made me do it! Ha, ha!' Well, at EXCELLENT WAY, we are here to serve our guests with excellence. 'The Customer first' is more than a slogan to us. Customers are the reason for our existence. As the great Henry Ford said, 'if we are not customer driven, nor will our cars be!'"

THE GREAT AWAKENING

Oscar continued, "Let's talk about The Great Awakening. I believe that the Great Awakening in the 21st century for businesses is Customer-Retention Management. The bottom line is in a competitive global market, if you don't take care of your customer, someone else will!

THE GOSPEL OF CUSTOMER SERVICE

"We are committed to making a difference by taking care of our customers. We call it 'The Gospel of Customer Service.' Take a look at the screen." The first power point heading read, "THE GREAT AWAKENING OF THE 21ST CENTURY: THE C.R.M. WAVE!"

Oscar explained, "Customer-Retention Management has become The Great Awakening in the 21st century. Smart business owners have awakened to know that it costs six times as much to gain new customers as it costs to retain old ones. We must make the commitment, as my good friend John Williams says, to building relationships that last with our customers. What is your attitude about retaining customers?"

Here are some statistics to consider:

> ## Why Businesses Lose Customers:
>
> - *1% Died*
> - *3% Moved away*
> - *5% Influenced by friends*
> - *9% Lured away by competition*
> - *14% Dissatisfied with products*
> - *68% Turned away by an attitude of indifference on the part of a company employee*

Oscar continued with an emphasis on service by saying, "Customers desire delightful service. What makes service delightful? Here are some one-word answers: Unexpected, Undeserved and Unnecessary! These are service values that let the customer know that the organization really cares! The Gospel of Customer Service is quite simply this: ordinary people doing ordinary things extraordinarily well!"

Oscar's timer started to beep and he said, "It's break time. Let's take 15 minutes to go outside and get some fresh air, order a cappuccino from the dealership's deli downstairs, or just stay here in the training room and enjoy the music."

After the break, Oscar welcomed the class back. He began by saying, "The Gospel of Customer Service guarantees increase in any business, but first we must understand the nature of the customer."

Oscar then walked briskly across the room, smiled at the group, flipped the sheet on a large flipchart and said, "Let's get some understanding of who our customer is:"

THE GOSPEL OF CUSTOMER SERVICE

WHO IS MY CUSTOMER?

- The lawyer calls him a CLIENT.
- The doctor calls him a PATIENT.
- The hotel calls him a GUEST.
- The editor calls him a SUBSCRIBER.
- The broadcaster calls him a LISTENER-VIEWER.
- The retailer calls him a SHOPPER.
- The educator calls him a STUDENT.
- The manufacturer calls him a DEALER.
- The politician calls him a VOTER.
- The banker calls him a DEPOSITOR/BORROWER.
- The sports promoter calls him a FAN.
- The railroad executive calls him a PASSENGER.
- The minister calls him a MEMBER.

"The customer is the person that comes to us for products, services or solutions. The customer is the reason for the organization's existence!"

THE GOSPEL OF CUSTOMER SERVICE

"We are here to serve. If you don't understand the root, or nature of the concept of serving, you will offer only a surface type of service. You will only serve for what you can get out of the experience. Service is actually a spiritual concept. What does it mean to serve?"

> "We are Ladies and Gentlemen Serving Ladies and Gentlemen"
> — The Ritz Carlton

"The Ritz Carlton is known for outstanding customer service." Oscar pointed to the poster that emphasized their motto of serving ladies and gentlemen. "Service can better be understood by going back to the original Greek language." He then said, "I know a little Greek; he runs a delicatessen down town. On a more serious note, according to Strong's Exhaustive Concordance, the Greek word for serve (douleuo) means to be a slave."

This word serve comes from two Greek words: doulos and subservience.
doulos = subjection or subservience (either volunteer or in-volunteer)
Subservience = sub means below and literally means to get below and serve.

After this in-depth word study, Oscar asked the group, "Do you need a break? I'm sure your brain needs it after that word-study session."

The group responded, "Keep on. This is interesting stuff."

Oscar said, "Thanks for the compliment, but we will take a break. I believe that the mind can endure no longer than the behind."

After these training instructions, Oscar and the trainees took a break to get some fresh air and walk around the grounds. Several of the trainees went outside and walked across the lawn to gaze at the ducks in a beautiful man-made lake out front. While standing there, a flock of honking Canadian geese came in for a landing in a nearly perfect V-formation. Joe silently watched the geese and admired the beauty of this event as he experienced an inward sensation, wondering what this meant, if anything particular.

THE GOSPEL OF CUSTOMER SERVICE

CHAPTER 8

"DESTINED FOR GREATNESS"

After the break Oscar said, "Welcome back! Now, let's get practical about the power of service to make you great."

Joe raised his hand and asked, "How often do you folks see the geese land on the lake out front?"

Oscar said, "Only occasionally. All of the team members love to see that. It reminds them of my Gung Ho workshop!"

"Gung Ho?" asked Joe. "What is that?"

Oscar said, "Go pick up Ken Blanchard's book that bears the name Gung Ho and come back and tell me."

Oscar asked the group if they know that they are destined for greatness.

Joe asked, "How can you say that everyone is destined for greatness? I know that people like Michael Jordan, Tiger Woods and Madonna were destined for greatness, but how do you know we are?"

"It's real simple when you understand the rewards of true service. Dr. Albert Schweitzer, missionary and former head of hospitals in Africa, said, 'There is no higher religion than human service. To work for the common good is the greatest religion!' The word religion has its root in a Latin word meaning to bind together. Of all human endeavors, service has the greatest power to bind our lives together, to make our lives whole and to give our lives meaning. James in the Bible said that true religion is to serve!"

"The long and the short of it is: Service is the key to greatness and we can all be of service, so we can all be great."

> "The tragedy of mankind is not this or that calamity, but the waste of man's potential for greatness!"
>
> - William E. Channing

THE GOSPEL OF CUSTOMER SERVICE

"Your success in life or business will be in direct proportion to what you do after you do what is expected of you. This is called 'going the extra mile.' Great service organizations like the Ritz Carlton Hotel have learned this concept. They have even developed a corporate university to ingrain the attitude of outstanding service into its culture. The Ritz Carlton has three simple steps of service: The first step is to give a warm and sincere greeting. Use the guest's name, if and whenever possible. The second step is to focus on anticipation and compliance with guests' needs. The final step is to bid a fond farewell. Give them a warm good-bye, and once again use their name if and whenever possible." At this point, Oscar referred to the training manual and read, "Every part of the facility, every staff member and every product or process that bears the organization's name reflects the level of respect you have for service to your guests and team members. Service is the key to greatness!"

Oscar introduced this to the group and Joe said out loud, "Wow! That's first class. Customer service is challenging and exciting!"

Oscar said, "Amen, Joe!"

Before we take a break, I want you to look at my favorite quote on service and greatness.

Let's all read it out loud:
'Service Makes the Great Great!'

> **Greatness!**
> No one achieves greatness without first being of service.
> Service is the essence of greatness.
> All great men and women become great because they gave some talent or ability in service to others.
> And no matter how small our talent,
> We, too, can contribute in some way to others.
> We, too, can become great!

Oscar then walked over to the stereo system in the training room, put in an upbeat CD and declared, "Guess what, gang? It's break time!"

THE GOSPEL OF CUSTOMER SERVICE

CREATING RAVING FANS!

After the break, Oscar began, "I am not a namedropper, but I am a personal friend with Dr. Ken Blanchard, the author of the classic book Raving Fans—Revolutionary Customer Service. I spent two weeks in his home at his personal invitation. That was one of the greatest experiences of my life. Ken and Margie are real people. Ken has said it well. 'The most important product in every business is customer service. People remember great service, and unfortunately, they remember poor service even more.' Customer service is just as much a part of business as the product being sold. The golden rule for every business is simple: Put yourself in the customer's place.

"Remember, excellent service consists of ordinary people doing ordinary things in extraordinary ways! It takes an instant to stop doing the less-than-excellent thing and a lifetime of practice to maintain doing the excellent. It is in practicing excellence in the small things that you prepare yourself to handle the major things with quality!"

"Now take a look at your training manuals."

The page read, "Excellence in Service." The Apostle of Customer Service explained that an organization's ability to maintain a reputation for high levels of service excellence is the key to its continued prosperity and success. He then pointed to the next power point screen:

> No matter what you do in our organization, your job title is Problem Solver and your job function is Customer Service Excellence.

Oscar asked the group, "Will service be as important to our economy tomorrow as it is today?" He answered for them. "No! IT WILL BE EVEN MORE IMPORTANT! By all indications, the increasing shift from industrial America to service America—the demand for better and better services and the increasing number of service jobs—will make us all more service conscious. This will happen not only in America, but also around the developed world. Every team member can aspire to higher standards of personal and corporate excellence. The major challenge in taking care of the customer is to never become so good at it that you can quit working on it. Being of service is a process that you will be perfecting for the rest of your life!"

Oscar then said to the trainees, "Being extraordinary demands commitment. You must become a student of service and read and observe all that you can about those who have based their lives on empowering others. You must also work on developing good service habits, one by one. You can start today. Pick the first less-than-excellent thing that you are going to stop doing and the first excellent thing that you are going to start practicing. Track your new habits as they develop. Always give your best to the people you serve."

THE GOSPEL OF CUSTOMER SERVICE

"Let's talk about taking it to the next level in customer service. The saying, 'Take it to the next level,' has become a buzz phrase in the corporate world. C.E.O.s and corporate leadership are constantly challenging the executives and middle managers to develop strategies to take the organization to the next level. Often, the only reason to get to the next level is for more money. The key to the next level is simple. It is making an absolute Commitment to Excellence as it pertains to customer service."

Joe asked, "Are you saying that we should commit to excellent service because the customer is always right?"

Oscar said, "Here is my take on that: Right or wrong, the customer is always right."

"We make the commitment because it is the right thing to do. We are committed to serving our customers with excellence, whether they are right or wrong in our thinking; they are always right!"

> "When a customer enters my store, FORGET ME. He is king!"

"As you commit to the concepts of excellent customer service, great things begin to happen. The Gospel of Customer Service means a no-compromised commitment to serve our guests. To be the best, we must offer the best possible service in our organizations."

Oscar took a pointer from the training table, pointed to the board and said, "Now we need to understand the two types of customers: (1) internal customers and (2) external customers. Internal customers are anybody within the organization that depends on us for service. External customers are people who pay for our products and services. To deliver outstanding customer service, we must understand the purpose of a business. The purpose of every business is to create and to keep a customer. The best businesses take it to a higher level by working to keep internal and external customers."

MOMENTS OF TRUTH
...the truth shall make you free.

Oscar explained to the trainees that The Gospel of Customer Service demands that we understand the power of Moments of Truth. "A moment of truth is any critical moment in customer service. The following phrase describes it well: ' A moment of truth is anytime a customer comes in contact with any aspect of our business, however remote, and has an opportunity to form an impression.'"

"So you must be aware of all of the subtle opportunities you have everyday for impressing positively and all of the not-so-subtle opportunities you have for impressing negatively. Creating the right impression can be as simple as treating people the way you want to be treated or as difficult as treating them that way, even though they are not cooperative. Every moment of truth is an opportunity to create a moment of magic! Some physical moments of truth are: your building, parking lot and sales materials. Some personal moments of truth are: telephone manners, warmth, and responsiveness to customer requests. The rule with moments of truth is Everything Counts!" Oscar concluded the session on Moments of Truth by explaining that most customers today experience many moments of misery. "It is the norm to experience moments of mediocrity. The Gospel of Customer Service causes guests to experience moments of magic!"

CHAPTER 9

"THE THREE SPIRITUAL PRINCIPLES"

After lunch the class spent some time with Oscar, discussing what they had learned in the morning sessions and talking about how it applied in the work place at EXCELLENT WAY AUTOMOTIVE GROUP. After a vigorous discussion, Oscar said, "Now I know you have had a delicious lunch, but give me your best as we focus on the three core principles of how to operate in the Gospel of Customer Service. If you need to, get a cup of coffee and let's get the show on the road."

Joe said, "I can handle a cup" and offered to serve the rest of the class. Oscar took him up on it and promptly thanked him for the piping hot shot of espresso from the dealership's coffee machine. "Ah! Coffee is good!" said Oscar.

"We will now start to cover the first of the Three Simple Spiritual Principles for operating in the Gospel of Customer Service. Acting in sync with these concepts will release the awesome power of service excellence in our organization and in any organization. They are:

> 1. *A Meaningful Service Vision*
> 2. *Customer-Oriented People*
> 3. *Customer-Friendly Systems*

Joe immediately thought, That sounds familiar, as his mind raced back to the service at Zack's positive, upbeat church. Vision, People and Systems. The trainer then had everyone repeat after him three times, "Vision, People and Systems" and said, "Remember, repetition is the mother of skill and the seed of learning!"

THE GOSPEL OF CUSTOMER SERVICE

SPRITUAL PRINCIPLE #1:

"A Meaninful Service VISION"

Where there is no vision, the people perish...

"Now that we have a basic philosophy of service, let's tap into the three spiritual principles of the Gospel of Customer Service. These concepts, when properly implemented, will turn any organization into a customer service powerhouse.

"Principle number one is a meaningful service vision. Some of you are wondering, why vision first? It's simple when you understand it. Nothing significant happens until it is first a vision. Vision is the inner picture of what you want to build or become.

"You must create a vision of delivering extraordinary customer service to your customers. All great customer service starts with a clear vision or understanding of what great service looks like. Vision is a mental picture of a future state. It is a picture of how you see the organization performing. It is a picture of what you want to be when you grow up. Vision is seeing the end result, or the OUTCOME! Why start with a vision? Three powerful reasons:

1. *Vision creates focus!*
2. *Vision identifies direction!*
3. *Vision unleashes power!*

"Vision causes you to see the outcome you want in serving your customers. How do you want them to feel? What do you want them to think about your organization? What do you want them to say to others? You must imagine what perfection—centered on the customer—looks like."

"A great visionary illustration of the Gospel of Customer Service is the old classic story of the goose that laid the golden eggs. While taking care of the goose, which is analogous with production capability, the farmer's focus or vision was pure; so he reaped a harvest of golden eggs. Greed then took over and filled his visionary capacity. Greed became his focus. What happened when greed took over? The farmer killed the goose to get the eggs out all at once. The result was a dead goose and no more golden eggs. The customer, or guest, is like the goose that lays the golden eggs. Greed will always cause us to focus on the production (eggs of gold) rather than serving the goose, the source of the golden eggs. If you don't take care of the goose (your customers or guests), one day you will find a shortage of golden eggs (money). Many customer service people 'kill the goose' daily by not taking great care of the

THE GOSPEL OF CUSTOMER SERVICE

customer, and then they cannot seem to understand what happened to their golden eggs. In traditional religious work, we often call a time of fasting and prayer for financial breakthrough when the root of our problem is mediocre customer service!"

Remember, the customer is the reason for the organization. Take a look at the power point screen:

> **Four Levels of Customer Service:**
>
> 1. Customer satisfaction—The minimum requirement for survival.
> 2. Customer expectations exceeded—The minimum requirement for growth.
> 3. Customer delighted!—The chief aim of world-class organizations.
> 4. CUSTOMER IN WONDER AND AMAZEMENT! The goal of The Gospel of Customer Service and the key to rapid growth and profitability.

A VISION OF EXCELLENCE

"Vision may sound hyper-spiritual, but it is hard-nosed business sense to start with a vision. Look at this screen. Every great customer service organization started with vision."

- J. Willard Marriott - Marriott Hotels
- John W. Nordstrom - Nordstrom
- Sam Walton - Wal-Mart
- William Hewlett & David Packard - Hewlett Packard
- Thomas Watson, Sr. - IBM
- Walt Disney - Disneyland, Disney World Theme Parks

Oscar reminded his class, "At EXCELLENT WAY AUTOMOTIVE GROUP, we have a vision of service excellence. We call it the Gospel of Customer Service! Remember that the word gospel means good news, and it is certainly good news to have our customers become raving fans so we hear Ka-ching! Ka-ching! Ka-ching! We don't abuse our customers and make lame excuses like, 'The devil made me do it!'"

THE GOSPEL OF CUSTOMER SERVICE

Write the vision and make it plain on tables that he may run that reads it.
Oscar pointed to a success poster on the wall and said, "Even Aristotle taught excellence. He said,

---

EXCELLENCE

"Excellence is an act won by training and habituation. We do not act rightly because we have virtue or excellence, but rather we have those because we have acted rightly. We are what we repeatedly do. Excellence, then, is not an act, but a habit."
— Aristotle

"We believe that love is excellence in action. We endeavor to serve our guests with love. That's where we derive the name EXCELLENT WAY."

Joe thought this was pretty clever. "Sir?" asked Joe. "Have you ever read Tom Peters' book, In Search Of Excellence? I thought you adapted the name from that classic."

Oscar said, "Tom has a fine book and I read it many years ago, but the word excellence has always intrigued me, wherever I hear it. I saved my resources to buy my first three used automobiles. I then incorporated the name EXCELLENT WAY, and the rest is history."

"Wow! You have over one hundred acres of inventory and facilities here. You mean all of this started with just three vehicles?"

"No, it actually started with a VISION and a lot of help from the Lord, called the power to get wealth."
Joe thought to himself, What a concept!

VISION DEMANDS IMAGINATION

Oscar asked the class to listen closely as he said, "IMAGINATION – the greatest nation in the world! A great service vision is often a result of using your creative imagination to develop a customer-friendly vision. Take a moment and imagine a world evangelized with the Gospel of Customer Service excellence and saturated with excellent customer service. Get a vision!"

... And now nothing shall be restrained from them, which they have imagined to do.
Genesis 11: 6

THE GOSPEL OF CUSTOMER SERVICE

> **"Imagine"**
>
> Some people look at things that are and ask "Why?"
> I Imagine things that aren't and ask "Why not?"
> - George Bernard Shaw

COMMITMENT TO SERVICE

Oscar explained to the trainees, "We have learned that a company with a vision of customer service excellence believes that it exists to serve the customer. Vision means a Commitment to Service!" "Dedicate yourself to learning the essential practices of committed service and make a commitment to incorporate these practices into the work of the organization. The key is the staff's freedom to focus on the vision: customer service excellence under all circumstances!" Oscar said, "Let's get a lesson from Wal-Mart. Sam Walton, the founder and builder of the Wal-Mart empire, had his vision right! He said, 'The real boss is always the customer. And he can fire us at anytime by simply deciding to spend his money somewhere else.'

"Understand that you are the source of your customer service vision, because your vision is birthed out of your values! What are your real values?" Oscar then shared with the group a stack of little blue cards. "Here is a values-based vision builder. I call it the Gospel of Customer Service motto." The card read:

> Always do more than is expected of you.
> Always go the extra mile.
> If you do, customers will remember you, tell others about you
> and come back again and again!

THE GOSPEL OF CUSTOMER SERVICE

VALUES-BASED VISION

"One of my favorite quotes is 'The difference between ordinary and extraordinary is that little extra!' Extraordinary customer service goes way beyond the norm. A meaningful service vision will make you extraordinary. Because the service is extraordinary, customers will talk about it. As customers talk about the service, it sets a standard for the associates of the company, including its leadership, to live up to. It also establishes a benchmark for the industry and eventually for business in general! At EXCELLENT WAY AUTOMOTIVE GROUP, we have learned by precept and practice that service only becomes significant when it is so meaningful to your customers that they articulate and proclaim it! We have found that great values are critical to a great vision."

Oscar explained it this way. "A great vision contains three basic ingredients: (1) a vision or vision statement, (2) a mission or mission statement and (3) values listed in rank order. Values must be ranked or employees won't know what is more or less important when trying to make a decision that relates to the customer. At EXCELLENT WAY, our values are clearly defined and in rank order. They are: (1) Excellence (2) Effectiveness and (3) Extraordinary Results. All of our people know that excellence—which is love manifested in quality and distinction—is first. Love comes first because love never fails."

"VALUES are the foundation for vision. Here are ten possible values as an example of a values list. To be effective, an organization must choose three to five top values.
The following words are examples of core values that an organization can choose. They are Love, Integrity, Success, Excellence, Winning, Hard work, Intelligence, Morality, Service and Effectiveness." Oscar looked the group over and said, "Let's take a brief break before lunch. I don't want you to drift and miss this critical lesson."

Oscar welcomed the class back with a little name-that-tune trivia by playing a small section of a popular 70s tune. He then gave a box of See's Chocolates to the winner. "Now that I have your attention, let's get back to the knitting."

"General market research reveals that it costs six times as much to get new customers as it does to keep old ones. If you are serious about customers, you should think deeply on that statement of fact! You could say that the success of your organization is determined by your quality ranking in the marketplace. 'Quality' is defined by the product or service, plus the way it is delivered. Wisdom dictates that we make our organizations and services of the highest possible quality!" Oscar then asked the trainees to write a short paragraph on what they thought was quality customer service, after which they had a great time of discussion. Oscar then shared that a 100% commitment to quality delivery is a must; Toyota is one company that has proven that with their kaizen philosophy of constant and

THE GOSPEL OF CUSTOMER SERVICE

continuous improvement. Oscar then said

"Never compromise quality in products or services!"
"Great session! Let's break!"

TOM TREADWELL

After returning to class, Oscar said, "I learned years ago that teaching is telling, but training is showing. This afternoon I want to show you a real life example of how the power of vision can transform a person from being a car dog to being a customer service pro. We are going to visit one of our best service writers, Tom Treadwell, in the EXCELLENT WAY service department. Tom Treadwell, AKA 'Terrific Tom' will show you where the rubber meets the road in our vision."
Joe said, "That sounds like fun."
Oscar told the trainees to leave their books in the training room, but to be sure to bring a pen and notebook. They all headed joyfully down the stairwell to the service department.

As the group entered the busy, beautiful air-conditioned service department, one trainee said, "This is no ordinary shop and this floor is so clean you could eat off it."
A bubbly, tall, handsome, dark-haired gentleman came dashing out from behind a counter and said, "It's A GREAT DAY AT EXCELLENT WAY! I'm Tom Treadwell. How can I be of service to you all?"
Oscar stepped out of the group and said, "Hi Tom. I have some new recruits to whom we are showing the WAY."
"Oh, Mr. Paywell, I didn't see you. This is the class I met at orientation. At first I thought I had a tour group from one of our local colleges coming through again."
Oscar said, "Thanks Tom, but just call me Oscar. I want you to take a little time as usual and tell these people about the transforming power of vision. I'll be back in about forty-five minutes. I have an interview waiting. Gotta keep the pipeline filled with good people, you know."
"At your service Mr., oops, I mean, Oscar. They are in good hands with Treadwell."

Tom turned to the class and said, "One of the first things I had to learn when I came here to work was the power of a vision to transform your heart. I have now been here for ten years. I had worked for five other dealerships over a span of four years and learned all of the bad habits you can imagine. I was truly what we call in our industry a 'car dog.' Mad at the world and ready to bite, scream or cuss when I felt that a customer was trying to get the upper hand on me."

Joe asked, "How did you change?"

THE GOSPEL OF CUSTOMER SERVICE

Tom answered, "The Great Awakening! The Apostle and the Gospel of Customer Service caused me to awaken to treating customer's right. This awareness of my way helped me change to the more excellent way. You could say I saw the light and repented!"

"Oscar did a class back in those days called 'Transformation Training.' First he taught about the heart. A change of heart is often the birth of a vision. This is a change from the inside out. The change is a desire to serve people. You See it, Size it and then Seize it! Then he said that the change affects your head. You think about it constantly. Finally it affects your hands. You start to use your heart, head and hands to serve your guests with excellence."

Tom then told the class that there is a customer service crisis from coast to coast. "The word crisis to the Chinese means danger; yet opportunity. We have a great opportunity today by offering extraordinary service, since service everywhere is so bad."

"Service in most car dealerships and businesses is so bad today that people expect to be abused. Have you had any poor service lately?"
Several in the group nodded "yes" and others said out loud, "Sure have!"
"Here are some areas of mediocre service that are almost the norm: dirty restrooms, late deliveries, lost product orders, unkind cashiers, rude greeters, lazy staff and broken promises. At EXCELLENT WAY, we focus on operating in The Gospel of Customer Service which gives us a definite edge in the 21st century."

We don't want satisfied customers, but AMAZED customers!

THE RIGHT VISION

"At EXCELLENT WAY AUTOMOTIVE GROUP, we are big fans of Dr. Ken Blanchard. In fact, it was his book Raving Fans and his FAITHWALK Leadership Program that really got Oscar turned on to the theory of serving customers. We call Raving Fans our customer-service Bible. It is required reading for all of our employees. Ken has a part in every excellence award we have ever won.
"Dr. Blanchard has another excellent book written with Jesse Stoner entitled, Full Steam Ahead. This book makes 'the vision thing' plain. In it, Ken says the three key elements of a compelling vision are: First, significant purpose; second, clear values; third, a picture of the future."

"The Power of the Right Vision does several things. It attracts commitment and energizes people, creates meaning in workers' lives, establishes a standard of excellence and bridges the present and the future."

Tom moved to a large poster saying, "Here is an example of an empowering Vision:"

THE GOSPEL OF CUSTOMER SERVICE

> **Our Vision**
> To Be An Ever-Expanding And Vital Market Vehicle For Use By God To Work In The Lives Of People As They Serve And Contribute To Others.
>
> ServiceMaster®

VISION OF PERFECTION

"I always strive for perfection when dealing with my service guests on the service drive. To be the best, you must strive for perfection. Some say, 'Lighten up on perfection. Nobody's perfect.' Here is something I learned at a training class that will help."

Why Perfection?
Let's say perfection is 100%. Even 99.9% would NOT be good enough.

Why? If 99.9% were good enough:

- 22,000 checks will be deducted from the wrong bank account in the next 60 minutes.
- 1,314 phone calls will be displaced by telecommunication services every minute.
- 12 babies will be given to the wrong parents each day.
- 268,500 defective tires will be shipped this year.
- 20,000 incorrect drug prescriptions will be written in the next 12 months.

"Customer-contact people must use their own imagination in conjunction with management to create a vision of perfection that fits within the organization's structure and is based on the customer's needs. "Always remember, you must pursue perfection to achieve excellence!"

This builds self-esteem and it's fun! Resolve to give the best customer service of any person or organization in the world. Decide what excellent customer service would be and get started."

THE GOSPEL OF CUSTOMER SERVICE

"Customer-contact people must use their own imagination in conjunction with management to create a vision of perfection that fits within the organization's structure and is based on the customer's needs. "Always remember, you must pursue perfection to achieve excellence!"

This builds self-esteem and it's fun! Resolve to give the best customer service of any person or organization in the world. Decide what excellent customer service would be and get started."

Tom told the class, "It's been about forty-five minutes and you can bet your bottom dollar that Oscar will be coming down any minute now."

Joe Simple said, "I am amazed at how in-sync you are with Oscar and his teachings, and how in-tune this whole place is with this interesting church I attended months ago with a friend."

Tom said, "That's the transforming power of catching, carrying and communicating a vision. When people have the same vision, they are 'in-sync,' as you put it, Joe."

"Now," Tom said, "Oscar has taught us five practical steps that I want to share with you. This is a critical piece of information that I call 'vision action steps.'"

1. Develop and communicate a clear vision.
2. Make certain that no jobs are labeled "Customer Service." Service is everyone's job.
3. Train all staff members in customer-service basics.
4. Keep the vision of service excellence before you and your people!
5. Passionately pursue perfection!

LEXUS
"The Passionate Pursuit of Perfection!"

While he was still chatting, Oscar came bouncing in and said, "Thanks, Tom, for your investment in our new class. Your labor is not in vain."

"You're welcome, boss."

THE GOSPEL OF CUSTOMER SERVICE

Oscar took the class back up to the training room and dismissed them for the day. Another wonderful day, Joe thought as he headed to his BMW to hit the local Starbucks.

As Joe walked into Starbucks, he looked on the wall above the counter in the workers' line of sight and saw a poster that read,

"For some reason, your customers seem to get better when you get better!"

Joe thought this was very interesting. I'm seeing this customer service excellence stuff everywhere I go now! I believe I am catching the VISION!

SUMMARY of Spiritual Principle #1:

A Meaningful Service Vision

- Service starts with a vision
- Create a clear vision of perfection, centered on the customer
- Vision must align with values
- A clear vision puts us in sync with others
- You must catch, carry and communicate the vision

THE GOSPEL OF CUSTOMER SERVICE

CHAPTER 10

"TRAINING DAY - TWO"

Spiritual Principle #2:

Customer-Oriented PEOPLE

Oscar welcomed the group with an energetic, "Good morning! Now I want to teach you how to be a COP (customer-oriented person).

"It's time to get into the heart of the Gospel of Customer Service by looking closely at the second principle. We call it 'Customer-Oriented People.' Walt Disney said, 'You can dream, create, design and build the most wonderful place in the world, but it requires people to make the dream a reality.' Amen, Walt!"

"Customer-oriented people have a radical, fanatical and relentless focus on the customer! At EXCELLENT WAY, we only hire customer-oriented people. We don't hire people whom we have to tell to be nice to the customer. We hire nice people! Why? You must understand and serve the desires of the customer to win in today's competitive marketplace. The Gospel of Customer Service will give the customer service rep understanding and insight into what customers generally want."

Here are some vital questions to ask yourself:
- Who are your key customers today?
- In the future?
- What are their expectations for service quality?

"You must discover the customer's vision and then alter your vision, if need be." Oscar said, "We teach and train our people to always remember this: Doing things well that are not important to the customer has no impact!"

> "You Can Dream, Create, Design And Build The Most Wonderful Place In The World, But It Requires People To Make The Dream A Reality."
>
> — Walt Disney

THE GOSPEL OF CUSTOMER SERVICE

Oscar then asked the class, "How do you find out what customers want?"
One trainee said, "Study market trends."
Another said, "Examine buying habits."
Joe said, "This may sound super-simple, but ask them!"

"Mr. Simple, you are simply brilliant! It's so simple that most MBA students miss that one. Always remember, you have not because you ask not."

"Let me illustrate. I was watching our own Atlanta Falcons play the Cleveland Browns in a pre-season game and the commentator was asking the V.P. of Marketing, 'How did you guys make history by selling out the Falcons season?' His response blew me away. He said, 'Arthur Blank simply asked the fans what they wanted and tried to accommodate them.' The result? A sold-out Georgia Dome and the Falcons are leading the league in team sportswear sales."

Oscar said, "That sure isn't rocket science, is it? Here are some sample questions. Ask, 'How can we better serve you?' You can also ask, 'How can we improve our services in the future?' When they answer, always say, 'We'll get on that right away!'"

Oscar sat down on the training table and said, "Let's have a heart to heart about relating to customers in a friendship relationship. I call this 'customers and you.' Customer retention is the key to organizational success. Customer retention is what we call a 'critical success factor.' Single visit guests are too hard and expensive to acquire. Your focus must be on the second and third visit. The organization's goal: resale to the same customer over and over. Customer retention is a major key to continued growth of a business or ministry. In the automobile business, most of my colleagues have a saying that there are no such things as be-backs! A be-back is a customer that did not buy, but instead promised he would be back. Many, even humorously; yet seriously, say the be-back bus has broken down. At EXCELLENT WAY, we have a 65% be-back closing ratio (be-backs that bought automobiles). We believe in be-back and repeat buyers."

Here are some samples of what customers want:

- FRIENDLY, CHEERFUL SERVICE
- PROMPTNESS OF SERVICE, DELIVERY AND BILLING
- EASE OF TRANSACTIONS
- CONVENIENCE AND NO HASSLE

THE GOSPEL OF CUSTOMER SERVICE

"They also want to receive quick responses to problems and complaints, to be valued and appreciated and to be made to feel important. This can only be accomplished with customer-oriented people. Service legends have learned to set minimum standards for customer service and hire customer-friendly people." So be a COP! If you want to make customers happy! Happy customers = Kaching!!!

THE POWER OF WOM!

Oscar continued. "Customer-oriented people who relate to the customer in a positive manner release THE POWER OF W.O.M. (Word Of Mouth)."

"Negative talk that is true is especially damaging to an organization. Word of Mouth is the major influence in the market today. Word of mouth, what people are saying about your business, is the most powerful and inexpensive source of advertising. Your aim is to deliver with such excellence that customers begin bragging about you, which then releases the power of WOM."

"Your method: Customer Service Excellence by speedy response to inquiries, fast action on complaints, regular follow-up and continuous service. WOW!"

"Our major measure of success at EXCELLENT WAY is the percentage of business we obtain from repeat sales and referrals that are sent by our previous customers. Imagine if a company could not market or advertise anymore. What would happen to the business? The key to getting repeat and referral business is to treat every customer as if you were on the verge of losing him or her!

Customers that are treated like kings and queens by customer-oriented people become fans of the business. I'm amazed by the amount of businesses that can't see this. I think they are blinded by the cash bottom line. I like what Ken Blanchard teaches about the bottom line. It's smart stuff. Ken says with passion that there's a triple bottom line: Gung Ho people that act like they own the place, Raving Fan Customers that brag about the organization and Big Bucks—financial profitability. Here are some reasons for customer defection: lack of attention, indifference on the part of someone in the company, lack of responsiveness to inquiries, and lack of responsiveness to complaints. Remember, fast response builds loyalty!" Oscar then said, "Check out this concept."

Golden Rule: Serve your customers the way you would like to be served!

Golden Chain: Develop an endless chain of referrals and repeat customers.

THE GOSPEL OF CUSTOMER SERVICE

"USAA (United States Automobile Association) is a great example of excellent customer service through customer-friendly people. They have come out with ten PRIDE principles that all of their employees know and live by:

1. Exceed customer expectations.
2. Live the Golden Rule.
3. Be a leader.
4. Participate and contribute.
5. Pursue Excellence.
6. Work as a team.
7. Share knowledge.
8. Keep it simple.
9. Listen and communicate.
10. Have fun!

Oscar then said to his trainees, "The big question you must answer is this: What do your customers think about your service and people? If you are in business, this is the most important question you can answer! As you can plainly see, the customer could be your best critic if only you would let them speak up! The fact is, most customers don't take the time to let someone know when they are unhappy. They harbor resentment and at some they point simply choose to take their business somewhere else."

"A statistic I want you to always remember is this: For every customer that complains, twenty-six do not! It is imperative that you understand what your customers think and what they expect from you. Remember, it is their choice to do business with you. Research reveals that you must make the customer feel at ease about complaining if you want honest feedback." After this intense session Oscar said, "Some of you are starting to get that glazed-over look."
"Oh no, we are just soaking in the seriousness of customer service," Joe said. "As you were speaking, I was thinking that the way I treat customers affects everything in my life, including my five-year-old daughter's college education. This is great content. I would have never expected this quality of training in a car dealership."
Oscar then said, "Thanks for your kind comments, Joe. All right! Take a break, get a bottle of water and a piece of fruit or beef jerky from the training snack table and I'll see you in fifteen minutes."
After the workshop, nobody moved from their seats, so Oscar looked the group over and started singing the McDonald's jingle, "You deserve a break today… I'll see you…"

THE GOSPEL OF CUSTOMER SERVICE

Upon returning from the break, Oscar said, "I have a gift for the person that can tell me the three spiritual principles of the gospel of customer service. Please raise your hands." Joe quickly raised his hand, stood up and said:

> 1. Meaningful Service **VISION**
> 2. Customer-Oriented **PEOPLE**
> 3. Customer-Friendly **SYSTEMS**

Oscar said, "That's excellent Joe! Here's a twenty-five dollar gift certificate to Starbucks Coffee!"

Joe said, "Mama Mia! STARBUCKS! It pays to pay attention!"

Oscar said, "Remember class—Vision, People and Systems. I like it! I like it! I think you are getting it now! I want you to drive home today saying, Vision, People and Systems!"

One student said, "I find it easy to remember things in threes, just like lions and tigers and bears; what does that make you guys think about?"

"The Wiz," said a young trainee who had not said a word until now "The Wizard of Oz is our family favorite and my dad said he has watched it since he was a tot."

Oscar said with a smile, "If you can remember that, you can remember the three principles of service excellence."

The young student said, "Yeah, but I've seen the Wizard of Oz fifty times."

Oscar said, "Hint, hint. Repetition is the seed of learning and the mother of skill!"

Vision! People! Systems!

THE GOSPEL OF CUSTOMER SERVICE

A CULTURE SHOCK!

"Your corporate culture has everything to do with how customer-oriented your people are. Even if you bring customer-oriented people into a bad culture, they are often brought down by the negativity. Here are five steps to transform your culture into a customer service giant. We eat, drink and breathe these at EXCELLENT WAY!"

1. Create the culture you desire.
How clear are your standards on which behaviors and attitudes are acceptable?
Most employees are willing to do what is asked of them, as long as it is reasonable.
The grumpy boss coming down on others for a poor attitude toward customers is the ultimate oxymoron! The key to your culture is WALK YOUR TALK!
2. Empower your staff!
Knowledge. The more people understand about the company, its philosophies, marketing strategies and goals, the more effective they will be in delivering the level of service you desire. Do the organization's employees understand the vision, mission and values? Do they know what it costs to acquire a new customer?
3. Provide skill-development training.
Most companies do not train their staff in customer-service skills.
Most people have never been taught or trained in people skills (the basics of human relationships). Customer service is all about human relationships.
4. Coach everyone!
Communication is the key to success! It is crucial that employees and managers have a clear understanding of their performance expectations and how they are going to achieve them. Reinforce positive behaviors and modify negative behaviors.
5. Repeat the sounding praise!
An environment of praise is conducive to customer service excellence.
An environment of criticism is counter-productive to great customer service!
The major principle here is what Dr. Ken Blanchard calls Gung Ho! A Gung Ho environment is charged with enthusiasm and energy and the energy will be transferred to the customer. To have Raving Fan customers, you must first have Gung Ho people!

"As customer-oriented people, we continually focus on what customers want and need. We are intensely focused on the customer. You could say that we truly care about people. People are the key to customer service, not inventory systems or fancy computers. People!

THE GOSPEL OF CUSTOMER SERVICE

"I had done several speeches on customer service for what I consider a truly great life insurance company, New York Life. When I was engaged in my due diligence in preparing for my first speech in their Atlanta office, I found the key to their greatness. They have a customer-oriented vision and mission that they live by. Check this out and notice how customer oriented it is:

> **New York Life**
> **VISION**
> To Make New York Life The Company You Keep!
>
> **MISSION**
> Every decision we make, every action we take has one overriding purpose:
> To be here for our customers when they need us....

"If this is not customer-oriented, I'll be a monkey's uncle! I was even more impressed when I saw their values. Here we go....

> **New York Life**
> **VALUES**
> Financial strength
> Integrity
> Humanity; *treating customers, agents, and employees with compassion, consideration, and respect.*

"I love the fact that humanity is one of their values! The focus is on people. Taking care of people's needs, customers and agents.

"Customers come in with needs and people meet those needs by friendly service, use of tools and use of technology, but don't lose sight of the human factor. At EXCELLENT WAY, our people are truly our greatest asset. Not our elaborate building, our multi-million dollar inventory or our state of the art computer system. People, folks—individuals! One by one, many companies let people go by the hundreds every year to protect the owner's yacht fund or some other material perk of the top dogs! People serve customers, not things. Just ask Sam Walton, Walt Disney or Thomas Watson Sr. (IBM's founder). Read about these service legends if you are serious about outstanding service. I think

THE GOSPEL OF CUSTOMER SERVICE

those giants would turn over in their graves is they saw how poor customer service has gotten. Woe to the customer-service agent or so-called business that abuses the customer on purpose and just keeps saying, 'The devil made me do it!'

I think some people should be arrested for customer abuse!"

"Henry Royce, the creator of the Rolls-Royce automobile, once heard a technician who was working on a difficult problem say, 'That's good enough.' Some reports say that some of the other workers had to physically hold Mr. Royce off the man. For Mr. Royce, nothing was 'good enough!' That's a man with a passion for serving people. I want to shout it in the market, in the C.E.O.'s conference room and in the sales meetings, 'People, People, People!' Profit is the applause you get when you take care of people! As Sly would say, 'Everyday people!'"

One student said, "Oscar, I think you missed your calling—hint, hint." Oscar just smiled real big. He then put on a humorous professional voice and said, "Empirical studies and profound knowledge give us the intellectual insight that customers often determine how good you are, based on regular, ongoing service."

Research reveals that the following factors are important to customers:

- Quality at every turn
- Solutions to problems
- Solve customer needs
- Solve and deal with confrontations
- Quick responses. Be quick to respond.
- Be at your post! Customers hate arriving at a counter and not finding any help.
- Excellent service after the sale.

> "At most car dealerships, the most abused customer is the 'sold' customer. We are 100% committed to excellent service after the sale!"
> Bernard Smalls

THE GOSPEL OF CUSTOMER SERVICE

GETTING INTO YOUR CUSTOMER'S SOUL

"At EXCELLENT WAY, we have learned that it is crucial to get into your customer's soul and make sure you are doing a good job!"
Joe said, "The word 'soul' just seems a little strong for customer service. Isn't there a better, softer word we can use?"
Oscar responded, "Actually Joe, the word 'soul' does not mean what most people think. Some people think of soul music and get images of Tina Turner rocking the house. Religious people think of the eternal human spirit. The word soul means mind, will and emotions. Does this make more sense now?"
Joe said, "Yeah, you got me for a moment. Thanks for the clarity."
"How do you get into the customer's soul? You ask them for honest feedback and the customer tells you. Another way is to do surveys or questionnaires. Ask specific questions. Don't just ask questions like, 'Are you happy?' Get specific!

Here are some sample questions to ask:
What are your expectations of us? How are we doing?
How can I increase the value of my service today?
The most important question to improve on: If you could think of one thing that could have made it even better, what would it be?
Then you must listen…

Be swift to hear, slow to speak…

NO MORE LOYALTY?

Oscar said "Many business leaders and managers are saying there is no more loyalty in the marketplace, especially in the automobile business. But I have found that you can create loyal customers if you know how to use your resources and turn dissatisfaction into loyalty. There is a key to loyalty. Here it is: Loyalty in today's competitive market must be created! Pull out you're thinking caps and let's be creative."
- How can you recognize your customers in special, personalized ways?
- In what ways have you been able to implement customer service innovation in your job?
- How could your organization's customer service become more ideal?
- Do everything in your power to solve the problem immediately.

THE GOSPEL OF CUSTOMER SERVICE

"Use the 'I think this is the best way' method. It's better than, 'This is the only way.' Do something extra for the customer. After you solve the problem, do something more. If possible, do something extraordinary. Remember, questions are the greatest customer-service tool. The better you become at asking questions, the easier it will be for you to become a customer-service pro and create loyalty. The better you are at asking questions and listening, the more you understand the customer."

Oscar walked to his large flipchart and displayed the sheet that read:

> **"Seek first to understand, then to be understood…"**
> *— Steven Covey, 7 Habits of Highly Effective People —*

"In designing services, we need to remember above all else that our logic is not necessarily the same as the customer's logic. Losing sight of the customer's logic can cause your organization to become introverted, to have employees who don't understand the services they deliver in holistic terms and who easily get caught up in methods and procedures and lose sight of the effect their organizational apparatus has on the customer. Insisting that your customer follow complicated procedures for the benefit of the organization is dumb!

> **"THE CUSTOMER'S PERCEPTION IS EVERYTHING!"**

SOLUTIONS CREATE LOYALTY

Oscar went on to say that "To create loyalty, you must understand that customers want solutions above all else. Here are five factors in the execution of solutions."
1. You must choose the best solution—always and without fail.
2. Use the word "recommend." Tailor the recommendation to the customer's needs, not to your own.
3. Give the customer confidence—not so much because of your knowledge about policies or procedures, but because you are able to access what you know and apply it in terms and services that are meaningful to the customer.
4. Involve your customer in the solution.

THE GOSPEL OF CUSTOMER SERVICE

5. Don't use technical or spiritual terms. The customer wants simple, straightforward solutions and not Greek, Hebrew or Hi-tech terms.

"At EXCELLENT WAY, we always treat customer complaints with the utmost urgency. Most customers believe that we as dealers are all about sales and not service, so our attention to details concerning customer complaints makes us stand out from the pack." Oscar said, "I love this job!"

"We teach and train our people that no matter what happens, continue to make your customers feel important. Never let the customer think you have anything more important to do than to be with him or her at that moment, especially as you move toward the conclusion of your conversation. Pay special attention to small details. Little, apparently insignificant differences between your organization and your competitors can mean everything. Recognize and capitalize your slight edge through fanatical attention to details."

Remember, "God [or the devil] is in the details…"

CUSTOMERS WANT STRONGER RELATIONSHIPS

Oscar said, "Now that we have a pretty good handle on the principle of complaint resolutions, we need to know and remember that relationships count! Research reveals that most customers want stronger relationships with the people they do business with. This creates the trust factor. Since there are so many products and services in the highly competitive marketplace, most customers are looking for someone they can trust. The friendship factor is one of the most powerful factors in business, especially in selling." As my good friend John Williams, the owner of the history- making Toyota Mall of Georgia, would say; 'We are here to build relationships that last with our customers.'"

> *"Seventy-one percent of people buy from you because they like you, respect you and trust you!"*
>
> *– New York Management Club Study*

THE GOSPEL OF CUSTOMER SERVICE

Oscar shared a story with the group about a friend who was a former pro-football player who had gone through a relationship-based training at his dealership, but moved away and went to work for a local dealership. The friend said to the interviewer, "I have been trained in relationship-based selling and…" Before he could finish the statement, the interviewing manger said, "Now listen! I don't go for that soft stuff. Our philosophy here is simple. Put the screws to them before they put the screws you."
Oscar continued, "My friend took the job out of desperation, but soon quit the dealership and went into another type of business."

Here are some simple ways to build stronger relationships:
- Manage the first impressions! You never get a second chance to make a first impression!
- Knowledge of your business! General knowledge (a little about a lot of things)!
- Enthusiasm!
- Imagination!

Oscar's timer started to beep and he said, "Let's take a well-deserved break! See you in fifteen minutes."

GEORGE GOODWRENCH

"All customer-oriented people have attitudes of excellence! To best communicate this, I want to take you all on a field trip to our parts department to meet George Goodwrench. George, like Tom Treadwell, is one of our customer service stars at EXCELLENT WAY. George Goodwrench will give you the nuts and bolts of tightening up your mental attitude. He is Mr. Positive Service Attitude. Let's go…"

As they walked into the parts department, they all noticed a motivational poster that said, "Attitudes of Excellence=Customer Service Excellence." A well-built, handsome, African-American man came out from his office when he saw a group gathering at the parts counter. With a bright smile he said, "It's a great day at EXCELLENT WAY! How can I serve you?" Oscar was purposefully hiding behind a pillar, so when he heard George's greeting, he popped out and said, "Surprise, George! I have a wonderful group of trainees for you to chat with. Remember, you met them at this week's orientation along with Tom and Sally?"

"Of course. How could I forget such a good-looking group?" said George. "They really cheered us on in the training room as shining stars."

Oscar said, "I need to go to the fitness center and check out the big screen Sony. Some of the workers say it went out during Sports Center late last night. We will have it repaired or replaced before the technicians and clean up crew get off so they can enjoy their workout more. I'll see you in about an hour. You are in 'good hands' with George.

George took the trainees into a big open area, pulled up a flip chart and started to share…

THE GOSPEL OF CUSTOMER SERVICE

ATTITUDES & ALTITUDES!

George said, "I really like to call this part of the training Attitudes & Altitudes. At EXCELLENT WAY AUTOMOTIVE GROUP, we believe that your attitude in customer service controls our altitude in the market place. I have found that most managers reprimand people and just say, 'Get your attitude right,' without ever really teaching and training frontline people in what a good attitude looks like. Remember that all excellent customer service starts with understanding what a good job looks like. Get this point guys: Your Attitude Controls Your Altitude!"

Frontline employees must develop an attitude of integrity. Integrity is authenticity, fairness, ethics and consistency. Many in our business believe that it is all about the money. We believe that money is a result of a wealth of character, ethics and principles. We embrace what Ken Blanchard said in his wonderful book, Big Bucks, 'Profit Is The Applause You Get for Taking Care of the Customers.'"

Joe said, "George, that sounds good, but how do you operate in integrity and not go broke in today's competitive markets? Everybody lies in business today; particularly when buying or selling a car. In the I.T. business my old boss used to operate in situational integrity. Meaning, he told the truth as long as it didn't cost him a deal or a contract. He would say, 'That's the way it is because business is business!'"

George said to Joe, "I appreciate your honesty. Many in the automotive business believe that if you can't let lies roll off your tongue with a straight face, you just aren't a good car man. They feel that a good liar is synonymous with a good car man. But we are the number one volume dealer in Atlanta, and all of our deals are integrity based. We believe in the old saying, 'The truth will always outlive a lie.' To give real service, you must add something which cannot be bought or measured with money, and that is sincerity and integrity."

THE GOSPEL OF CUSTOMER SERVICE

INTEGRITY BASED SERVICE

Here are some principles on how to express integrity in service:
1. Commitment to the win-win dynamic. If something is good for the customer, it has to be good for the organization.
2. High productivity. When you love what you do, you find the energy to do it well.
3. High quality. If your heart is in something, you will do your best with the highest possible standards.
4. High standards. If you pursue integrity in all that you do, you will not slack off.
5. Lots of fun. Can you have passion without enthusiasm? Enthusiasm means to be imbued with spirit—God within. If God is within your conscience, you will have an inward pull toward integrity. When you operate by integrity, it won't be dull.
6. Consistency without conformity. Adherence to a strong set of standards which promote ownership and creativity.
7. Have your heart in your work and your work in your heart!

> *We are in business for one reason: to serve society!*

FRONTLINE ATTITUDES

George then moved back to another chart that read, The Attitude of Personal Excellence must be developed because you do not inherently put the customer first!
Frontline Employees are the key to great customer service because problems are best solved at the point of the problem. "Outstanding Customer Service demands that you go the extra mile with the right mental attitude. Attitudes control altitudes! Edison said, 'Greatness is an ordinary man with an extraordinary attitude!' Now, let's focus on this attitude/altitudes concept in some specific areas that we need to work on."

"The first attitude that needs to be developed is Attitude in the Workplace. The glad attitude is contagious in the workplace. I firmly believe that what Wally "Famous" Amos said is true. He said, 'Whatever you see on the screen of life was first seen in your mind. If you don't like what you see, change the reel of film, change your attitude and change your thoughts.' We need to renew the spirit of our mind by developing a fresh mental and spiritual attitude. To truly be happy, you must do what you love and love what you do! Ken Blanchard says, 'If you want to make Big Bucks, love thy work or try Las Vegas!'"

THE GOSPEL OF CUSTOMER SERVICE

"Happiness in the workplace is the major key to providing superior customer service. None of this training works to its maximum potential without happiness in the workplace. Service is demanding. Service inherently breaks down if those delivering it are not happy. People need to be given space to provide truly outstanding customer service. Managers must encourage growth and then give people room to grow. Support and encouragement are a mental safety net for happiness. Give people room to be outstanding!"

"The second attitude we want to look at is the Attitude of Teamwork."

George then said to the group, "We must come to value The Wisdom of Teams. Start to use the terminology "Our Company." I'm sure that some of you have studied psychology at one time or another. In just about any good book on empirical psychology you will find 'Maslow's Hierarchy of Human Needs.' Abraham Maslow taught that humans have five basic needs that fall into an order or hierarchy: 1) physiology 2) safety 3) social 4) self-esteem and (raise next line here)5) self-actualization. Self-actualization is becoming all you should be and is the highest need of humans. It also relates to belonging to something great and serving others. We are really here to serve others. That is where we find our greatest fulfillment, or 'self-actualization,' as Maslow puts it. Belonging to something grand is the greatest of human needs. Develop team thinking in the workplace!"

Here are some team-building principles:

• Give others what they want first. People will generally work hard for emotional benefits and recognition, in addition to the monetary income.

• Show respect for others. The courtesy you express to other team members generally sets the example for the respect you show to your customers.

• Make other team members feel important. Human Resource professionals insist that as much as 90% of things we do in life are fueled by a desire to feel important. Seek ways to be a genuine cheerleader.

• Offer positive feedback. William James, one of the world's best-known psychologists, once said, "The desire to be appreciated is one of the deepest drives in human nature."

• Do simple favors for others. The Harvard Business School conducted an extensive test to determine how successful people earn the respect and cooperation of their coworkers. They found that one of the most effective techniques—developing a knack for doing simple favors—was the easiest and least costly.

• Use names. This has been mentioned previously in terms of your conversations with external customers. This should certainly be in your relationships with team members!

THE GOSPEL OF CUSTOMER SERVICE

"The third, and final, attitude to develop is the Attitude of a Peace Maker."

Joe said, "Now come on, George. That sounds a little too spiritual for the workplace. In a results-driven numbers game like the car business, who has time to be a peacemaker? I was taught to get it done and then be a pacemaker."

"Well Joe, the Book says 'Blessed are the peacemakers,' not the pacemakers." I must say that in our industry, most car dogs only care about numbers and cash. In many dealerships, you can have the owner's firstborn if you sell enough cars for him. We believe that our business is empowered to prosper when our people avoid getting into internal politics and strife, which comes from trying to climb the ladder of sales at the expense of positive relationships in the workplace. We are a business, but we are also a team and a family, if you will. The Book also says in James 3: 16, 'For where envy and strife is, there is confusion and every evil work.' When you get into politics and strife, you will not be thinking about the customer, but about yourself."

Three types of employees that will not serve customers well:

1. **Politicians** – *striving for recognition and promotion*
2. **Egotist** – *blinded by self interests*
3. **Freeloaders** – *looking for a free lunch.*

"The fatal flaw in customer service is selfishness! It is being so focused on what you want to happen that you lose sight of what the customer wants to happen. Selfish people carry a negative mental attitude! Zig Ziglar says, 'It's your attitude, not your aptitude that controls your altitude!'"

Joe said to George, "I understand where you are coming from with all this attitude stuff, but my understanding of the car business is that it's a cash cow. You milk it for money. We sell cars for money, don't we? The bottom line is money. I was taught back in New Jersey that there are three reasons to go to work: money, money and money!"

George said, "You know, Joe, I am a musician and we did an opening once for The O'Jays. The first song they did that night was the 70s oldie but goodie, 'Money, Money, Money.' Great beat; great music. A timeless proverb says, 'Loving favor is more valuable than silver or gold.' In fact, if you are the best, you will gain the favor of your customers and have all the gold you want. Remember that the goose lays the golden egg! Zig Ziglar certainly understood this when he said, 'You can get anything in life that you want if you just help enough people get what they want!'"

THE GOSPEL OF CUSTOMER SERVICE

George said, "Let me ask you folks a question. Does anyone here know what makes most customer service representatives outstanding?"

    John said, "Raving Fan Service?"

    "Good try, John."

    Jill said, "An extraordinary attitude?"

    "Excellent thought, Jill."

    Joe said, "From my training, I believe it's communication skills."

    "Bingo! You got it, Joe. Now let's study how to be outstanding in customer service." George then said, "Just having a positive attitude is not enough to serve customers well. This will help put attitudes into action." George began to give the trainees a list of ***The Three V's for Better Communications:***

    "The First V is Visual. Remember, you get no second chance to make a first impression. Clothes don't make the man, but they sure do introduce him. Before you have had a chance to say a word, many people will judge you strictly by your appearance. Your choice of clothing should be suitable for the situation. Always look professional. Never look sloppy!"

    "The Second V is Vocal. Remember, the way you sound in person or on the phone has an impact. Have you ever listened to a monotone? We all have a vocal range to work with. Our range rises when we are stressed or under pressure. Most customers prefer listening to calm, lower-pitched voices. We can all learn to speak this way."

    "The Third V is Verbal. To wrap it up on communication, let's talk some about Verbal skills. Look in the training manual with me at Verbal Communication Rules: Use descriptive language. Use short sentences. Avoid slang, technical words and jargon. Avoid tag questions and qualifiers (I guess, probably, sort of, etc.)."

    We have found at EXCELLENT WAY that having short and informal conversations with customers can be an effective way to add a friendly touch to your interactions with them. It shows that you are a warm human being and not a robotic customer service representative. Some topics to avoid are controversial subjects like:

Politics
Religion
Ethnic jokes
Salaries
Rumors
Gossip
Confidential business information
Negative information about competitors

THE GOSPEL OF CUSTOMER SERVICE

Oscar had finished with the big screen task in the fitness center and came in to find the class standing around George as he discussed the importance of communication skills. George said, "Let's do a quick checkup from the neck up by analyzing how to change your customer service attitude. To improve on your attitude, you must become a believer. If necessary you must repent and believe the Gospel of Customer Service. You'll see it when you believe it."

George said, "Now, let's go all the way with PMA (Positive Mental Attitude)! As I said, the boss is back, so I will bow out. Here's Oscar!" The group gave him a standing O.

Oscar asked the trainees, "Did George do a good job with his attitude workshop?" They responded, one by one and together, "Yeah, wonderful, awesome, great!"

"Well, let's go back up to the training room and wrap it up."

Oscar turned to George and said, "You are certainly making a difference here at EXCELLENT WAY, George. Well done! Keep up the good work."

"Thanks boss. All the way with PMA!"

As they entered the training room, the trainees found one of the waitresses from the deli standing by a portable ice cream maker. "Ice cream to end the day for anyone? We have many different flavors and different types of cones."

Joe said, "I'll take cappuccino on a chocolate waffle cone."

Others started to pipe in their orders. One young lady in the group turned to Oscar and said, "Thanks Mr. Paywell. You have a way of making us feel so special."

Oscar smiled and said softly, "You are special!"

Oscar said, as they were enjoying the gourmet ice cream, "I have one thought before leaving. Dale Carnegie said, 'When dealing with people, remember you are not dealing with creatures of logic, but with creatures of emotion—creatures bristling with prejudice and motivated by pride and vanity.'"

"Remember the way you have been served during this training class and do so unto others. Operating in the Gospel of Customer Service means having customers fall in love with our people and our organization so they begin to brag about us to their family, friends and associates! Let's go home. It's been a great day!"

THE GOSPEL OF CUSTOMER SERVICE

SUMMARY of Spiritual Principle #2:
Customer-Oriented People

- *Hire nice people*

- *Learn to listen to customers*

- *If customers are not happy, they are just looking for a way out and they won't come back unless there is nothing better.*

- *Make sure your priorities are the same as the customers!*

- *Take care of your customers!*

THE GOSPEL OF CUSTOMER SERVICE

CHAPTER 11

"TRAINING DAY - THREE"

Spiritual Principle #3:

Customer-Friendly *SYSTEMS*

The next morning Oscar came happily into the class. He welcomed the group and said, "I'm excited to see you all again. Let's all stand up and say something positive to start the day! Repeat after me, I feel healthy, I feel happy, and I feel terrific!" All the trainees stood, widened with amazement, and repeated the chant. Joe had already heard this before on one of his W. Clement Stone tapes, so he just smiled and thought, Wow this is great! What a release of energy!

Oscar said, "It's day three, and today we will cover the final principle in the Gospel of Customer Service, which is Customer-Friendly Systems. Of the three major principles, you will see how customer-friendly systems allow you to deliver excellent service. Consistent systems cause consistent delivery which creates customers for life. The commitment is to design every part of your organization, with service as the desired outcome, so that you exceed the customers' expectations. Jesus taught the Biblical principle about going the extra mile. Customer service is a great opportunity for acting on this concept. In The Gospel of Customer Service, you must always go the extra-mile!"
"You have heard the old saying, 'The road to hell is paved with good intentions.' The road to poor performance is paved with the organizations intentions to serve the customer without customer-friendly systems! Good intentions are not enough. You must have systems. Systems control action. Action is the key. Just about any company and organization, secular or religious, will defend their intentions to take care of customers, but when I go in and watch their people I see the paved road of intentions, but little real action based on well thought-out customer friendly systems. Some systems are just plain dumb when it comes to customer service! Amen?"

The group said, "Amen!"

"Consistent delivery is a key customer retention strategy. Consistent delivery demands systems! The organization's major goal should be to deliver such excellent customer service that a solid relationship is developed with guests that return again and again. Customer-friendly systems will produce outstanding customer service, which in turn causes customers to return again and again!"

THE GOSPEL OF CUSTOMER SERVICE

"The only thing that makes our organization stand out from the crowd is The Gospel of Customer Service! Doesn't it make sense in an unstable economy to work harder to retain your customer base, in which you have invested thousands of dollars to develop?"

"The most valuable asset any company has is its customer base, yet many treat customer service like it's just a slogan. Slogans are okay, but we must go beyond slogans to systems that benefit the customer. Here is an example of a good-sounding slogan. Let's examine it."

"The Year of the Customer!"

Oscar said, "Now, let's do a little critical thinking. If this is the year of the customer, what will next year be? You must have systems and not just slogans, because in delivering customer service, even though you have good intentions, many things can go wrong because of the human element."

"All legendary service organizations have customer-friendly systems. They do the small things to provide a level of service that exceeds customer's expectations. Customer service people need the skills that empower them to take care of customers. Remember, they are the customer-contact people. They contact the customers that you spend advertising dollars on in order to draw them into your business. Many organizations, businesses and ministries need to rethink their training budget. Why spend thousands in advertising to have untrained people serve your guests?"

Oscar said to his trainees, "We at EXCELLENT WAY know that customer service is a very demanding job. Customers will put you under the microscope when they find that you preach the gospel of Excellent Customer Service. Why is customer service so demanding today? Customer service today is more challenging than ever before. Customers are more educated than ever before. Customers are more knowledgeable about products and services than ever before. Customers are more demanding with regard to quality, service and value. Customers have so many choices and less urgency to make decisions. Customers are impatient and want everything now."

THE GOSPEL OF CUSTOMER SERVICE

THE TEN COMMANDMENTS OF CUSTOMER FRIENDLY SYSTEMS
(Notice they are not the ten suggestions)

"Ten customer-friendly procedures to meet the demand are:

1) Listen to what customers say about your organization.
2) Involve the whole organization in the service process.
3) Respect the fact that customers vote most clearly with their patronage!
4) Hang out where your customers do.
5) Observe your customers being served by others.
6) Relate your customers' experiences to your own.
7) Organize opportunities to pay attention (focus groups, employee site visits)
8) Train the frontline to listen and communicate feedback.
9) Create the customer service point-of-view for all staff members.
10) Seek to exceed expectations!

SALLY SELLERS

Oscar said, "Now to bring service into perspective, I want to present to you our real expert in customer service. Her name is Sally Sellers, our top performing sales champion. Let's go downstairs to the sales floor and spend some time with her."

As they prepared to leave the training room, a tall, slender redhead with a pleasant smile came out of the elevator.

"Sally," Oscar said, "we were on our way to your work station."

Sally said, "I knew you would be coming, but I wanted to come to the training room to talk to the trainees and to give them my undivided attention. It is so busy down on the sales floor."

Oscar said, "Well, guys, grab a snack and let's take our seats. Sally is well worth listening to."

Sally said, "Being number one in sales in the 21st century demands that you have some quality customer service systems. Here is my threefold system and how it works."

Sally went to the board and wrote "A Threefold Customer Service System!"

THE GOSPEL OF CUSTOMER SERVICE

Sally pulled out three rubber balls and said, "Heads up guys!" She shouted, "Attitude!" as she threw a ball to Joe. Then she yelled "Art!" and threw a ball to a young trainee that happened to be named Arthur. Then she looked around the room and saw a 6'5" trainee named Big John and said, "This one is big!" She yelled, "Process!" as she threw the third ball to John. "Customer service is an attitude, an art and a process!"

> **The Threefold Customer Service System**
> - Attitude
> - Art
> - Process

Sally said, "The first part of the customer service system is Attitude. Your attitude is either a trap or it is a freedom. In my studies of the behavioral sciences I learned that people are not the creatures of circumstances, but rather circumstances are the creatures of people. I like that because that means I can create my own attitude!"

"Customer service is an Art and service should be creative! Use your creative imagination to enhance the service experience. There is no 100%, only close and closer. Service is a continuous creative pursuit. It's an art. The art of rapport is a crucial skill in the Gospel of Customer Service. Customer service agents must understand the basics of body language to build rapport with customers."

> **Research shows that of our communication:**
> - 7% comes from the words we use
> - 38% comes from our voice tonality (pitch and pace of words)
> - 55% comes from our physiology (body and posture)

Sally then said, "To be effective in the art of rapport, you must understand how to match and pace your customer in the areas of words, tone and physiology. This increases the customer's comfort level. Service is an art!

THE GOSPEL OF CUSTOMER SERVICE

"Finally, in the big three, we must understand that customer service is a Process! Service is a process. A process is a system. Finding the best way to do things is continuous. An effective process is the best way known to do a task. It brings order to the components of service. It leaves you free to concentrate on the finer things and add touches that make service come alive. It makes measuring progress possible, which is the key to continuous improvement. It facilitates consistency over a large and growing organization."

Sally then said to the group, "As a top performing sales consultant with the Southeast's fastest growing auto group, I have learned that to truly serve with excellence and to go for the gold, you need to constantly be challenging yourself to be extraordinary."

Sally said, "I love this quote: 'The difference between ordinary and extraordinary is that little extra.' Extraordinary service is the key to more customers, more sales and more profits: big bucks! How many times have you been treated poorly by a business in the last 30 days? KAIZEN is the Japanese philosophy about how one approaches work with continuous improvement (better, faster, more efficient ways of doing it). Challenge yourself to make improvements in your job and you will be motivated to achieve them. Kaizen will make you extraordinary!"

Sally said to the trainees, "Let's take a look at 12 Failure Systems for customer service organizations. By the way, Oscar does an excellent job of keeping us focused so we don't fall into these."

1. Desired inventory is not in stock.
2. Delivering no service or poor service after the sale.
3. Sales people who are poorly trained, uninformed or distracted.
4. Red tape and bureaucratic processes.
5. Making customers wait to get into finance or to spend money.
6. Tricky pricing—phony numbers marked on vehicles.
7. Misleading advertising—bait and switch tactics.
8. Value is not commensurate to the price of the automobile.
9. The parts department with poor quality products and accessories.
10. Owners failing to stand behind vehicles or services.
11. The dealership with poor housekeeping, dirt, disorder, safety hazards.
12. Inconvenience —location, layout, parking.

THE GOSPEL OF CUSTOMER SERVICE

Sally then said, "To be a shining star of service and remain number one in sales you must be committed to going the extra mile on doing what Ken Blanchard calls in his wonderful book Raving Fans, 'Deliver plus one%!' This means always give your customers more than they expect. Some call it under-promise/over-deliver. I agree with Ken and endeavor to deliver what I promise plus one %."

Joe thought to himself, She is a real disciple of Oscar. You can tell who she's been hanging around with!

> **KAIZEN**
> *Constant and Continuous Improvement!*
> *Kaizen will make you extraordinary…*
> *Kaizen will make you Big Bucks!*

Sally then said, "I don't need a crystal ball to give you this prophetic word. Here it is: Operate your business by these failure systems and I will predict your future—Failure! Failure systems produce failure. These twelve, when not handled properly, kill a business and its sales success."

Sally said, "I have a gift for you. Here it is: Good is the enemy of best! One giant in business, who is also a personal friend, often uses the phrase 'Best Practices.' In this concept, you look at what has worked and what has not worked in your industry (even borrowing from competitors). You simply eliminate the failure systems and adapt the success systems that give you the highest chance of success. You then ingrain these success systems into the corporate culture as a Best Practices training program. Best practices are a form of success system."

> **Best Practices!**
> *Good is the enemy of Best!*

Sally said, "Let's now look at one of my favorite parts of the whole program. One of the major ways to cut down on upset customers is to understand that Training Ingrains Systems. We must transform our information to add value to our customers by systematic training. Training ingrains systems into the corporate culture."

THE GOSPEL OF CUSTOMER SERVICE

8 Distinct Steps to Continuous Training

1. Align your values with your vision! Why am I doing this? Your work must have purpose and lead to a desired end result. Begin with the end in mind.
2. Learn to think strategically! Tactical, reactive work may not lead you to the desired end. A clearly defined mission statement or statement of goals is absolutely necessary to stay focused and reduce the clutter of everyday living and working.
3. Gather your resources! No one has enough time, money, people or information. What do you need to accomplish your mission? Stay flexible.
4. Manage your priorities every day! If you are working on anything that does not lead to your ultimate vision in life, Stop! You are wasting resources and limiting your personal effectiveness.
5. Measure your results. Is your customer base full of Raving Fans or satisfied customers? Ask them.
6. Take ownership of your work. How can you be effective if you don't? Personal responsibility=ownership. The attitude of ownership is unique.
7. Improve your ability to influence others. Command and control is either dead or dying in today's work place. You move ahead by discussing, selling, influencing, inspiring or convincing. Learn to deal with others as partners in a collaborative relationship.
8. No matter how well you do your job, improve on it everyday! "World class" means doing it better today than yesterday and better tomorrow than today. Sounds simple, but recognizing the demand of our new economy is one thing and resolving to do something to change it is another.

"Any business or organization that is not engaging in ongoing systematic training is not serious about customer service. Here at EXCELLENT WAY AUTOMOTIVE GROUP, we use this training room nearly every week of the year (except the week after the holiday season). We have an administrative assistant who schedules classes and issues calendars constantly. Most car dealerships use the training room as a lunch room and usually have outdated training materials stacked in the corner next to the Eddie Murphy videos that the guys watch for laughs while waiting for customers. We are staunch believers of ongoing training. You could say we are religious about it!"

THE GOSPEL OF CUSTOMER SERVICE

O THANK HEAVEN FOR SALLY'S SEVEN
"This is what I call SALLY'S SEVEN; they work!"

Here are Seven Tips that make up a Success System of Extraordinary Service:

1. Make Lasting First Impressions. From the moment potential customers walk through the door or call on the phone, they are making a decision whether or not they are going to do business with you. Greet the customer with enthusiasm and a smile and welcome them as you would a friend into your home.
2. Ask the customer. Ask them for suggestions on what you can do to improve your level of service. Ask them what other products or services they would like to see you carry in your store. Ask them for 3 reasons why they do business with you. It will send a clear message to the customer that you value their feedback.
3. Remember Special Dates. When was the last time any company that you have done business with remembered a special, significant date in your life? Build a profile on each customer. Ask them to provide you with birthdates and anniversaries. In recognition of their anniversary as a customer, send them a gift or card from the business.
4. Give Them Added Value. The average business spends six times as much money attracting new customers as it does retaining existing ones. Invest in your existing customers (customer appreciation day, free gifts, etc.). Show them that you care!
5. Show Appreciation. When was the last time you received a "thank you" note or a heartfelt "thank you" for spending your hard-earned money with a business? Look your customers in the eyes and say, "Thank you for doing business with me."
6. Keep In Touch With Your Customers. How often do you hear from the insurance agent that handles your insurance needs, the real-estate agent that sold you a house or the countless other businesses that have provided you with a product or a service?
7. Take Care of Your Customers. Whether it's the person stocking shelves or the person behind the cash register, taking care of customers is everyone's job!

THE GOSPEL OF CUSTOMER SERVICE

THE COMPLAINT DEPARTMENT

Sally then said, "To discover what the customer wants, you must train yourself to welcome customer complaints. Most customer service reps run from and avoid complaints. The fact is, if you want to create customers that brag about your service, you must pay close attention to complaints. The numbers tell us that 96% of unhappy customers who have a complaint won't complain (91% never return); for every complaint you get, there are 26 unhappy customers who you don't hear from; the typical dissatisfied customer will tell eight to ten people; 70% of complaining customers will do business again if you make an effort to make them happy; 90-95% or more will do business with you again if you jump through hoops to make them happy! This goes up to 96-97% if you solve their problem on the spot! Listening, without interrupting, is about 60% of the solution."

"Here is some of the best information I have found that you could use in understanding customer complaints."

Apathy: Some team members believe that their job is to shuffle paper and pound a computer keyboard. Our primary job should be to serve people (help people and offer good solutions).

Insolence: Sometimes we are a bit too proficient in brushing people off with standard procedures. It lets us off the hook, or so it seems, but causes less than ideal customer service.

Curtness: How many customers feel like they are an interruption to the customer service representative's day?

Patronization: Treating the customer poorly is hardly a way to encourage repeat business, but it is the norm in many businesses.

Routine: Team members who merely go through the motions are transparent to customers.

Run-arounds: Some customers get dizzy from being shifted from person to person.

Sally said, "I've developed a strategy that I use when dealing with a disappointed customer. Complaints are inevitable. Only responses are optional. Customer complaints are an opportunity."

Here is the complaint resolution strategy:
1. Hear it out completely.
2. Don't defend! Empathize—I understand how you feel. If I were in your situation, I would feel the same way.
3. Apologize—I'm sorry. Offer to resolve the problem immediately.
4. Make amends—Do something extra for the customer.

THE GOSPEL OF CUSTOMER SERVICE

Sally then pointed to a large poster on the back wall and said enthusiastically, "All customer service organizations understand this."

"There are only two things that any customer buys. First, they buy solutions to problems. Customers generally don't buy tangible products; they buy solutions! They want products for the problems that they solve. Second, they buy feelings. Customers want more than a product. They want to feel good about themselves. They also want to feel direct contact with you and your organization. In the final analysis, the success or failure of our organization depends on how many people we reward with those two things."

Now let's look into some reasons why customers get upset. Many businesses fail to understand that most customers get upset due to a lack of the company having a clearly-defined service strategy. I know that some customers get upset because they may be angry at life in general. There may be little you can do for such persons except listen. Research reveals that many get upset legitimately, due to an organization's lack of a clear strategy or lack of implementing the strategy they have on paper. The long and the short of it is that those customers believe that most mission statements are just wall plaques. Here are some factors that upset customers. You may bear the brunt of having associates who misrepresent things, are inept coworkers, don't have proper product knowledge, don't meet expectations, deliver less than is promised or who are either rude or indifferent. Think back to the main reason why customers switch. It is not because of price or product quality, but because of how they are treated. Customers have to wait. People hate to wait. We live in a fast paced world. Customers are often not taken seriously. If they have a complaint, they want to be noticed and acknowledged. Customers are sometimes embarrassed, and consequently, they act angry because they did something wrong. The key: always allow the customer to save face! The customer's integrity or honesty may have been challenged. Give the customer the benefit of the doubt. Somebody from your organization may have argued with the customer. There is no such thing as a win/lose situation. If the customer loses, we all lose. Perhaps the customer is incensed because he or she has been given rules, procedures or policies that limit what you can do for them. And the beat goes on... Your attitude must be to help them all you can."

GET THE PHONE!

Sally said, "To be a real customer-service pro, you must work on your phone skills. From the moment you reach for the phone, use it as a powerful tool. Don't fall into the trap of being sloppy over the phone just because people can't see you. They can sense your concern, or lack thereof. Make the telephone your ally and not your enemy! Remember, one customer who is served in an excellent

THE GOSPEL OF CUSTOMER SERVICE

manner can influence two hundred and fifty others to do business with you! This is the law of increase in motion! One customer who is abused, in person or on the phone, can influence as many as two hundred and fifty others (or more) not to do business with you. Since callers can't see you, your voice must feel welcoming. Enthusiasm, if genuine and warm, builds confidence. Limit your talking."

"Irate callers often have a lot of pent up frustration. Listen to them patiently and then they will be more likely to calm down and state real problems. Ask thoughtful questions. Probe, so you can feel and verbalize his or her complaints, wants, needs, desires, and wishes. Repeat the problem in the caller's words. By doing this, you provide valuable feedback. By using words as close to the caller's own as possible, you show that you truly grasp the problem and its implications."

"Concentrate on the caller's words and meanings. Give the customer your full attention. They can sense when you are distracted or bored. When they feel you are genuinely interested, they generally grow more amused. Offer encouragement. Use word tracts. Say, 'Exactly' or 'I understand what you are saying' or 'I can see how you feel.' Always thank the person for calling."

Oscar came in and smiled broadly. He was so proud of Sally that tears welled up in his eyes. She had come to his dealership broke and broken-hearted from a life of abuse. She was now truly a great one in customer service. She was a homeowner, a successful single mother of two teenage boys and a productive part of society. Oscar said, "Sally, you are my pride and joy! You are God's best!"

Joe said, "You sure are free with compliments."

Oscar replied, "Yes, Joe. We have created a culture where we don't hold back legitimate compliments. Cheering each other on as we work together is the gift of the goose. It's simply teamwork. We really care about each other in our dealership. It releases more energy, creativity and enthusiasm."

Joe's mind went back to the Canadian geese he had seen earlier, and thought, ah ha! Oscar then said to the class, "Let's take a fifteen-minute break and then I'll meet you upstairs to wrap up the day and the training program."

As soon as the calls began to break, Sally's cell phone started to ring. She answered it in her usual professional cheerful manner. "It's a Great Day, Sally Sellers speaking, how may I assist you?"

"Ms. Sellers, I hope I did not reach you at a bad time, but I have an emergency." "Who's calling, please?" asked Sally.

"Oh, I'm sorry. This is coach Schula, your son's high school football coach. Your son John has had what we believe to be a concussion. He was running a pass pattern and another player cut him off and blind-sided him. He took a pretty good lick to the head and we are on our way to the Garner emergency room."

THE GOSPEL OF CUSTOMER SERVICE

As soon as she told Oscar what was happening, Oscar got on his 2-way radio and had a porter deliver a car to the door. He told the class what had happened and said that he had to leave to take care of Sally and her son. Sally tried to discourage it, but Oscar insisted. He told the class, "I'll see you all tomorrow 9:00 a.m. and say a prayer for Sally's son." As the class dismissed one by one they told Sally how saddened they were by the incident. Sally thanked them as the porter came running in to let Oscar know that the car was ready.

Oscar opened the door for Sally and jumped in as they quietly raced toward the emergency room. As tear streamed down Sally's face, Oscar touched her hand and said, "It's going to be all right, Sally. Just hang in there."

They pulled up to the E/R to find that her son was still unconscious and connected to all kinds of medical equipment. Coach Shula welcomed them and gave his apologies.

Sally said, "It's not your fault; football is a tough game, but John loves it. He regularly says "Mom, one day when I am in the NFL I will buy you a new house, a new car, and you won't have to sell cars anymore—unless you want to." Sally wept. Oscar ran frantically around the hospital, making sure that everything that could be done was being done for John. A nurse came up to Sally and asked about insurance and Oscar stepped in ad said, "Excellent Way Automotive Group will stand with her 100% to see that the bill is fully taken care of. She has insurance with our company's group plan and if there is anything that the plan doesn't cover, I personally will. Let's just make sure John gets the best service."

As the night wore on, there was still no movement or word from John. Sally had no family in the area except the Excellent Way Automotive Group. She received call after call, checking to see if John was okay. Several employees showed up at the E/R, only to find that they could nt go into intensive care. By midnight Sally was worn out and sleepy; she sat back in a recliner to take a short nap. As she did, Oscar went over to John and grabbed his hand and started talking to his subconscious mind about his plans to play in the NFL, build his mother's new house, and so forth. Oscar whispered, "You have a wonderful career ahead of you and a lot of raving fans waiting to cheer you on. You must live..."

Oscar then closed his eyes. Seconds after he had said this, he felt the movement of John's hand. Oscar looked up and his eyes as they popped wide open and John said, "Mr. Paywell, what you are doing in my room?"

Oscar started to laugh and cry and he ran over and woke Sally up to share the good news. Sally leaped up and ran over to John, saying, "I knew he would be all right! I Knew it!"
The nurses came running in, asking what the commotion was about, when they looked over and saw John sitting straight up. The nurse said, "Settle down, please, while we do some tests. It can't be that he had a major concussion."

THE GOSPEL OF CUSTOMER SERVICE

After all of the tests, the doctor said, "I don't understand, but miraculously this boy is well. You can take him home after we do a few more tests, if all pans out." At 3:00 a.m. they drove away from the emergency room, with John not even having a headache. John explained to his mom and Oscar what happened as they all celebrated the outcome.

GOING THE EXTRA MILE

The next morning at 9:00 o'clock, the class was all asking about Sally and her son, showing their concern. Oscar told them that we had seen the miracle of hope, as he explained what happened as he spoke hope to John's subconscious mind. Oscar explained that the inner man never sleeps; he can receive messages even when the outer man is unconscious.

Joe thought to himself, far out stuff...

Oscar then said, "After we had sat there for hours in a hopeless situation, I thought I would speak hope to John's spirit, and it worked!"

"How late were you there?" asked Joe.

"We left the hospital at about 3:00 a.m."

"And you are here today?" asked a young female trainee. "I would be in Snoozeville."

Oscar said "I gave Sally the day off, but duty calls."

Joe said out loud, "Mr. Paywell you are definitely the Apostle of Customer Service!"

Oscar then said, "Now, back to training. We are going to deal with the strategies that will make you a customer service legend. Jesus called it 'going the extra mile.' I like to call it 'delivering more than you promise!' Don't drive promise down, but rather drive delivery up! Customer Expectations: meet first, exceed second. If you fall short of what you said you would do, the customer feels cheated."

"Here is a real life example of a poor system. I was at a car dealership recently, getting my wife's car serviced. It took the service writer about thirty minutes to complete the write-up for me to sign so I could leave. Granted, my wife did have a list of about five items. The real problem was in a flawed service system. The service writers were required to go out and inspect the cars coming in, write up the service order and answer the incoming calls. The guy received about three calls and proceeded to write up their service orders over the phone, while several paying customers stood impatiently in line. Requiring that they answer the phone is a part of a faulty service system. The man was a pleasant fellow, but he did not have a clue of the negative impact that this was having on me. I left and told a friend that if they were not the only manufacturer of the product in the area, I definitely wouldn't go back... We must analyze systems to make sure they are customer friendly!"

THE GOSPEL OF CUSTOMER SERVICE

Customer Friendly Systems

Every System Should Be Designed With One Person In Mind: The Customer!

Bernard Smalls

Oscar asked the trainees if they had learned anything.

They said, "More than we ever imagined in an orientation for a car dealership."

Joe said, "My neighbor went to work for a local family-owned dealership and he said the training program consisted of a stack of out-dated videos to take home and watch. However, this training program is first class!"

"Here is a critical success factor in customer service. All good customer service is the result of effective systems. Create happy customers by building systems that help you look after the customer's needs whenever possible. This whole three-day training program is about a system. To drive the point home, you could say that these three spiritual principles make a system of service. Let's look at them again:"

> 1. Meaningful Service Vision
> 2. Customer-Oriented People
> 3. Customer-Friendly Systems

"You must have systems. Become a fanatic of systems. Systems are what allow you to guarantee delivery instead of merely smiling and saying, 'Have a nice day.' A training program should ingrain the systems into the soul of the department. After training, you must establish your Performance Standards, which are the foundation of Customer Service Excellence."

- Train people to follow systems.
- Systems are not even worth a dime if people aren't trained to follow them.
- Deliver it time after time, without fail, in sync with the system.

Oscar flipped the page on his flip chart and said, "Check this out!"

THE GOSPEL OF CUSTOMER SERVICE

> At the core of every great customer service organization is a package of systems and a training program to inculcate those programs into the soul of the company.
>
> **Ken Blanchard, Raving Fans**

"With a rule, the emphasis is simply on procedure or policy and not the result. However, you must have rules. At a gas station, not smoking within ten feet of the pump is a good rule. Systems help to deliver service. Systems are predetermined ways to achieve results. The emphasis has to be on achieving the result and not on the system for the system's sake.

"Plays in sports are a type of system. The systems set guidelines, but sometimes you must enhance the play to score. The purpose for systems is to ensure consistency; not to create robots. Rules do that. Systems give you a floor; not a ceiling. Systems allow you to deliver a standard of performance consistently.

Systems bring order!

"You can't reduce great service to systems alone, but they are extremely important in the Gospel of Customer Service. A lot of companies have systems to extract cash from the customer's pocket, but I'm talking about excellent service that meets needs! Customers have needs beyond the company's product. People need to feel that they belong to a group. People need to feel that they are important. The Gospel of Customer Service must become a part of the company's culture, not a flavor of the month."

The Apostle of Customer Service now said, "When you get to the sum of customer service, it's really all about caring! If I could sum it all up, I would say that the Gospel of Customer Service is Caring!"

"Extraordinary customer service is always a result of efficient systems. Excellent customer service will be the key factor, not only in surviving, but also in prospering during the coming times of accelerated competition. In fact, customer care will soon become the business of businesses and not just for your organization, but for everyone."

"What is Customer Care? A sharp, clearly defined center of interest in delivering Ideal Customer Service! Focus on what customers need and want. Remember, the only reason for being and staying in business is customers."

THE GOSPEL OF CUSTOMER SERVICE

SUMMARY of Spiritual Principle #3
Customer-Friendly Systems

- Systems must be customer friendly
- Systems help you to deliver more than you promise
- Delivery is where the rubber meets the road
- Systems are vital
- Systems, not rules

Oscar concluded, "It has been great sharing these concepts with you all. I hope we have shared something that will help you to go out and make a difference, making the world a better place." Now it's time for a checkup from the neck up. It's time to test your customer service acumen. I have a fifteen question true or false quiz that will reinforce what you have learn and test your retention. Please write in T for true or F for false. Enjoy!

CUSTOMER SERVICE QUIZ

1. It is easier to attract new customers than to retain dissatisfied ones. _____
2. How you perform your job is a form of customer service. _____
3. You have no influence over whether a customer returns or not. _____
4. Most customers tell you when they are unhappy or upset. _____
5. It is more important to pay attention to new customers than existing ones. _____
6. The real boss is the customer. _____
7. Those who work behind the scenes are not in customer service. _____
8. When a customer has a problem, it is critical that they understand your point of view. _____
9. Customers can hear a smile over the phone. _____
10. Satisfied customers are not good enough in the 21st century. _____
11. Customer service can be difficult at times. _____
12. Profit is the reward you get for ripping off your customers. _____
13. Customers today generally have low trust in businesses. _____
14. Market research reveals that most customer who leave a business leave because of poor customer service. _____
15. Excellent service is the key to wealth, prosperity, and greatness. _____

(After you have completed the test, the answers can be found on page 115; don't peek, don't cheat)

THE GOSPEL OF CUSTOMER SERVICE

After collecting the test papers, Oscar said, "That was easy, wasn't it?"
One trainee who had been slipping in and out of focus during the three days said, "That depends…"
Oscar just looked at him and smiled, not saying a word.

"I will leave you with my final point. Always do more than what is expected of you. Always go the extra mile. If you do that, customers will remember you and come back. By the way, remember to fill out the evaluation form at the very end of the customer service training. At EXCELLENT WAY, we believe that feedback is the breakfast of champions!"

"Now let's all stand and say after me, 'IT'S A GREAT DAY AT EXCELLENT WAY!'
The group enthusiastically did so and Oscar gave them a big "God Bless you all!"

Joe Simple came up to thank Oscar for the life-changing training and to ask him a question he had wanted to ask ever since he had met Oscar, but for professional reasons had not.
"Oscar, do you mind if I ask where you attend to church?"
Oscar said, "No, not at all. I attend Creative Concepts Faith Centre in Suwanee, Georgia, a suburb of Atlanta. CCFC is a Bible teaching non-denominational church. The vision statement is 'Sharing a message of positive faith, helping humanity find purpose and significance.'" Joe thought to himself, Interesting. Reminds me of Zack's type of church. These new-style churches seem to be the bomb today, can't hurt to try it.
Oscar interrupted his thoughts and said, "Joe I'll give you a map." Oscar gave Joe the address and service times.

CHAPTER 12

"TGI - SUNDAY"
Again...

On the following Sunday, Joe drove into the parking lot of Creative Concepts to be met by a friendly parking lot attendant who opened the door of his BMW. "Good morning!" the young man said cheerfully.

Joe said, "Thanks" and went into the main auditorium. He thought, Everyone here is so nice; it reminds me of the customer service at EXCELLENT WAY.

After the praise and worship, Joe's jaw nearly hit the floor when the announcements were made and the assistant pastor said, "We will now have the Word for today from the pastor."

Joe thought, No! It can't be! As Oscar came to the platform, he waved and said, "Good Morning, congregation! Before we read our verse, let's all make our positive affirmation and shout, "THANK GOD IT'S SUNDAY!"

Joe was blown away and thought, This is amazing. During the training, he didn't tell me he was a minister. This is incredible.

After the powerful sermon on "Answering the Call to Wealth by Serving Others," Oscar gave an invitation for people to become believers in the religion of service. Hands went up all over the beautiful auditorium. Joe thought, I have heard enough. This is real. The gospel of customer service is not just for Sunday. It's for everyday. Joe said to himself,

> "True faith is about serving God through serving people everyday, in every possible way!"

After church, Oscar was greeting the first-time guests as they left, and Joe walked up to him with a beaming smile. "You are too much! Why didn't you tell me you were the minister when you invited me to church? Man you are good!"

THE GOSPEL OF CUSTOMER SERVICE

Oscar smiled real big, gave Joe a big hug and said, "God alone is Good! Welcome to the family of customer service, Joe!"

As they talked, Sally, Tom, and George all came seemingly out of nowhere to welcome Joe. Joe turned as pale as a sheet and asked, "What, is this some kind of a cult? What are you guys doing here?"

George said, "This is the spiritual service center. It's like a filling station. We come here on Sunday, get charged up, and go out into the Marketplace and serve. Oscar calls it 'spiritual pragmatism.' It is the real key to our cult-like service culture at Excellent Way Automotive Group. We come here and get blessed so we can go out and be a blessing to people. It's not a religion, it is reality. We are here to serve humanity. In the marketplace we do it with automotive solutions. Here we serve them with spiritual solutions."

Oscar said Joe, "I hope that through this experience you have seen the moral of the story."

Joe said, "Yes I have."

Oscar asked, "What is it?"

Joe replied, "The Gospel of Customer Service is not just for Sunday. It's about people serving people in every way, every day! Thank God it's Sunday!"

Oscar concluded by saying, "Remember the Gospel according to Nordstrom;

"This is what we are here for, to serve and to be kind!"

The Gospel According To Nordstrom
"THIS IS WHAT WE ARE HERE FOR, TO SERVE AND BE KIND!"

Bernard Smalls could be best defined as a servant-leader. He believes that the quality of a person's life is in direct proportion to their commitment to service excellence no matter what their chosen field of endeavor.

For great service, products, seminars or keynote speeches contact:

O. Bernard Smalls
P.O. Box 724
Suwanee, GA. 30024
email: bernard_smalls@yahoo.com

THE GOSPEL OF CUSTOMER SERVICE

Acknowledgements

Karen Smalls—my wife, my clover and my lover! Thanks for the years of faith in me…wow!

Alexia Smalls——my ten-year old daughter, for title cover design and font suggestions

Travian, Terrence, and Aaron——my three sons——destined for greatness…

Ken & Margie Blanchard--thanks for being pioneers and great examples of excellence

Dottie Walters—-Thanks for sharing your wonderful sprit and expertise.

Courtland E. Marchant—-my first customer service trainer in the school of hard knocks…

Jerome Smalls and Linda Taylor--for opening the door of opportunity to Blanchard Training & Development

John Williams—-The most motivated man I know. Thanks for allowing me to dance with the Giants!

Brian Allison—-Thanks for your belief in my training potential

Peter J. Daniels—-Thanks for loading my spiritual entrepreneurial shotgun!

The Southeast Automotive Group Team Members—-you are the best…

Toyota Mall Team Members…you are World Class!

Susan Massey—-for your editorial eye, and encouragement!

John W. Nordstrom, Walt Disney, J. Willard Marriott, Conrad Hilton, Sam Walton Sr., S Truett Cathy, Dr. Robert Schuller, William Hewlett & David Packard, Thomas Watson Sr. and all of the customer service gurus that helped shape my vision.

Last but first----The Lord Jesus Christ! My Best Friend!

THE GOSPEL OF CUSTOMER SERVICE

Answers to Quiz on page 109

1. False
2. True
3. False
4. False
5. False
6. True
7. False
8. False
9. True
10. True
11. True
12. False
13. True
14. True
15. True

Bernard Smalls is a Ken Blanchard Companies consulting resource who as corporate trainer helped make history at a Toyota franchise which was the first retail center to win every Toyota excellence award in the first your of business. Bernard is an Activity Vector Analysis analyst, a Predictive Index Analyst and a certified Situational Leadership trainer. Mr. Smalls holds a degree in Theology

Endorsements:

"In Thank God It's Sunday, Bernard Smalls delivers the good news that a serving heart is the key to prosperity. This uplifting parable—based on a true account of a wildly successful car dealership---shows that profit is the applause we get for taking care of our customers."
-- Ken Blanchard, co-author of The One Minute Manager and Raving Fans

"So many books are related to special systems to make production and profits in a mechanized way that suits and empowers the corporation. This new book of O. Bernard Smalls focuses in on the only real way of having business permanence: the customer. It is the customer that keeps a business alive, it is the customer that creates employment and it is the customer that is the only way to make a profit. 'Wake up corporations and appreciate and thank God for the customer.'"
-- Peter J. Daniels, Best Selling Author, Millionaire Real Estate Developer, and Australia's Top Motivational Speaker

"This brilliant book is like a hot cup of Java on a cold night. You will treasure it as I have and want to buy many copies to give to those you love. I highly recommend it."
-- Dottie Walters, CSP Author Speak and Grow Rich, President/CEO, Walters International Speakers Bureau

The Gospel of Customer Service

All Rights Reserved © 2010 by O. Bernard Smalls
No part of this book may be reproduced or transmitted in any form or by any means, graphic, electronic, or mechanical, including photocopying, recording, taping, or by any information storage retrieval system, without written permission of the author.

ISBN: 978-0-557-41313-3
Printed in the United States of America

www.ingramcontent.com/pod-product-compliance
Lightning Source LLC
Chambersburg PA
CBHW021006180526
45163CB00005B/1909